Narcissistic Wife

Learn to Master the Covert Narcissistic Personality Disorder in a Spouse, No Longer Be a Victim of Narcissistic Abuse in Your Marriage

Mona Diggins

Table of Contents

Introduction

"Empowerment is the ability to refine, improve and enhance your life without co-dependency."

Steve Maraboli

If you have ever been lambasted by a narcissist (which I'm assuming you have, since you are reading this book), you will know that it is easy to perceive them as heinous entities who are on the wrong side of all that is good in the world. Sometimes described as energy vampires, those on the receiving end of the narcissist's heartless endeavors might see them as soulless entities who are sharing the same space as you for the sole purpose of tormenting you and draining your energy. This kind of imagery is made especially easy to envisage if you are aware of the sort of vocabulary that is used to describe them in the mainstream media.

If you take the time to investigate some of the ongoing research about how these seemingly inhuman beings come to be, you will see that beyond the cold, selectively beguiling eyes of the narcissist is a wounded child who feels just as vulnerable and distrusting as we do, if not more so.

You will see later on that various theories attempt to explain the traits we associate with narcissism (lack of empathy and exaggerated sense of grandiosity, to name two of the most qualifying features). This can help you recognize the humanity in such people and try to take a more objective stance in the face of possible emotional and psychological abuse that you may interpret as being personal.

Before we dive into the oceanic depths of the mind of narcissists and start to map the landscape of their hearts, it's not easy to avoid the question of whether we should feel similarly sorry for narcissists as we do for the people that are buffeted around by their planetary-sized egos and manipulative tendencies. In a narrative that places the victim as the object of our sympathy, we have to ask: are they victims too? Do they deserve our sympathy? Of course, there may be a nugget of truth in the fact that the narcissist embodies many of the character traits we deem less than acceptable, immoral even, but this is beside the point.

The question of victimhood is relevant here because the purpose of this book is not to paint the image of the narcissist in a way that conforms to the mental pictures we already have from the bad rap they are given in the media. This may be unavoidable; as you know from your own experience, it is hard to argue with this kind of image if you have been on the receiving end of unrelenting criticism, to name just one of the many painful quirks of the power-hungry narcissist. It is rather to help you, having possibly taken the brunt of full-blown emotional abuse without knowing it, understand the narcissist in your life better, by shedding light on the complex myriad of factors that have collectively been involved in the development of narcissistic tendencies in your partner. Bear in mind that the intention in doing this is not so that you can compromise your own well-being to accommodate someone who has had a difficult time; it is rather to make available all the knowledge you need to help you to make informed decisions to help you to steer yourself toward good old-fashioned sanity.

On the other side of the coin, this book is also not intended to consolidate any feelings of victimization that you might have. Once you have become aware of the ways in which you have been treated that have been damaging to your mental health and general well-being, it may be tempting to want to appeal to people's sympathy and adopt the role of the victim.

The emphasis when talking about narcissists and how to ensure you retain your sense of self when you are around them is not so much about degrading them as it is about empowering yourself. That being said, this book aims to provide you with information, based on extensive research as well as my own experience living (and co-parenting) with a narcissist, that can help you gain insight into the psyche of narcissists in the context of the factors that have resulted in her being the way she is towards you. It will also provide you with the practical information you need to help identify narcissistic traits, give you the knowledge you need to enable you to recognize when your spouse is overstepping your boundaries as well as the tools and resources to do something constructive about it.

In this way, you will gain a greater understanding of the inner clockwork of the narcissist and what makes them tick. After reading this book, you should be able to recognize the antics employed by the narcissist in your life as they happen, in order to avoid unnecessarily wasting your energy on entertaining her whims and desires. The tools and techniques you will read about in this book will furthermore help you to return home to yourself, to draw upon your inner resources to retain your power and focus on your own needs. This will prevent you from being lured unsuspectingly into the narcissist's drama and being constantly drained by it.

So, what exactly can you expect from this book? Chapter one will provide you with anecdotes that can help you to identify whether your spouse is a narcissist, as well as provide you with a clear definition of what narcissism is. In chapter two, we will look more closely at Narcissistic Personality Disorder, the most extreme manifestation of narcissism on the spectrum as it is described in clinical psychiatry. Chapter three will examine in finer detail the different types and subtypes of narcissism—this can help you to recognize the nuances that define your partner's particular type of narcissism. Chapter four will lay out the causal factors that are presumed to be behind the development of narcissistic traits. The next chapter will explore the deeper processes that might be occurring in the mysterious mind of the narcissist, and the final chapter will describe a variety of red flags you should look out for, as well as helpful strategies you can use to help defend yourself against a narcissist and start creating a better life for yourself.

Recognizing the narcissistic tendencies in your wife that cut deeper than the facade she displays to gain approval from others, and being able to give the egotistical, selfish qualities in her the label of 'narcissist' is a major step in creating a more manageable, empowered life for yourself, and a happier environment for your kids (if you have any). To rise above the narrative she has created and gain a broader perspective that allows you to see the intricacies of your relationship that are unhealthy (and potentially abusive) is not an easy feat. It may seem callous and cruel to attribute the characteristics of 'narcissist' to her and to deflect her tactics in the ways suggested in this book. But while it might appear to be heartless at first, the intention behind the strategies you are adopting is ultimately care for yourself. By putting yourself first, laying down boundaries, and asserting yourself more through healthy communication, you will find that you are also better able to help others as well, instead of being the bad guy in a story that is fabricated by the wounded inner child of your spouse. Nobody likes being the bad guy, especially if it's not an accurate reflection of who you really are.

The idea behind this book is to help you explore and reflect upon yourself and your wife and the relationship you have, and to assist you in becoming conversant with the relevant vocabulary which, in turn, will help you to develop a deeper understanding of your wife in terms of how you can conquer, or at least deflect, her destructive and draining tendencies. Bear in mind when perusing this book that reading information can provide you with indispensable theoretical knowledge, but the more time you put into reflection, the better you will be able to practice integrating this knowledge into your personal life. It should also be mentioned that you can work through this book at your own pace and keep returning to it for future reference. This book serves as the beginning, or at least a contributing factor, to your creating a new life and support network for yourself that helps you to create a new, empowered story for yourself.

One of the major challenges in navigating the difficult and traumatic situation in your marriage is getting the support and resources that you need in the face of a structured system that is, frankly, designed to set you up for failure. It is helpful to get access to the perspectives of other people who have been in similar situations. Likewise, having resources that can help familiarize you with the useful strategies effectively used by others to unravel the knot that has you bound into a destructive and harmful marriage. This book is one resource you can draw from to help you keep returning to the irrefutable truth that, despite the opposing force in the 'harem' (the support system used by narcissists to validate the narrative they wish to create) and the seemingly insurmountable resistance in your circle of family and friends, you are not alone in your struggle. In building a new social network for yourself, one that is supportive of your empowerment in the face of adversity, you can start to root yourself in a new reality in which you are the writer behind the creation of your own beautiful life and story.

You are invited, as you work your way through this book, to be as active as possible in applying this knowledge to your own marriage. Engaging with the content can help you to integrate it into your everyday life—doing this will yield more results than if you motor through the chapters in an effort to finish the book as fast as possible. It is recommended that you take your time to familiarize yourself with the terminology, and reflect on how the information in each chapter applies to you, your spouse, and your marriage. In this way, you will be an active participant in the new life you are busy unfolding as you start taking the first steps in a new life by joining hands, hearts, and heads with those who have inspiring stories to tell about survival.

One final point before we get started. You may have read in the literature that most narcissists are men. It is also true that in most cases where the well-being of victims are seriously threatened in terms of safety or security, the narcissist is a man, largely due to the fact that men are physically stronger than women and, more often than not, are the main breadwinners in a family, or are at least considered as such. However, there are many cases in which the narcissistic spouse is a woman. Because this book is engineered to provide support to the partners of narcissistic women, I will be referring to narcissists as "she/her" rather than "he/him."

As we embark on the journey into the mental corridors of the narcissistic mind, laying out breadcrumbs like Hansel and Gretel in the woods is a pointless endeavor, as there is no turning back once you have read the perspectives offered here. But unlike these two fictional characters, pursuing this path leads to your liberation.

As a survivor of narcissistic abuse myself, I designed this book to help you realize that there are ways of navigating your marriage to a narcissist in proactive and constructive ways. So, are you ready to dig deep into the labyrinth of the narcissistic mind and be present with the resultant insecurities? If your mind is fertile for the possibility of meaningful change through the willingness to let go, work hard, and embrace the challenge of feeling the discomfort of taking back control of your life no matter what (or who) stands in your way, then proceed to chapter one and take a look for yourself at the reflection in the mirror.

Chapter 1:

The Reflection in the

Mirror

"Now I know what others have suffered from me, for I
burn with the love of my own self—and yet how can I
reach that loveliness that I see mirrored in the water?
But I cannot leave it. Only death can set me free."

Narcissus to himself in Edith Hamilton's *Mythology*

"One of the premier diagnoses of our times, narcissism
is a reflection not only of an apparent trend in mental
illness but also the strains and distortions in the lives of
essentially healthy people."

Robert Karen

It is impossible to avoid using the metaphor of a mirror
in a book on narcissism. It goes back to the Greek
myth of Narcissus, who was known to be the
embodiment of physical beauty. His mother was
warned by a wise woman that he would do well, if only
he would not become aware of his immense beauty.
But, as is the case with all stories that stand the test of
time, he did that very thing that he should not have. He
came upon the misfortune of seeing his image reflected

back to him in a pond, and he was so in love with his own reflection that he couldn't tear his eyes away from it. He spent the rest of his days gazing adoringly at himself and eventually drowned reaching for his face over the water, despite attempts by the nymph Echo to whisk him away from the folly of his own perpetual self-absorption and pursue a life of meaning and love.

I think we can all agree that the story of Narcissus can be interpreted as a love story gone horribly wrong. While it captures in the annals of time a valuable lesson for many of us, whether we are in a relationship with a narcissist or not, it is no accident that what we know as a narcissist today bears the same name as this tragic character. And it is no coincidence that the original person who bore this name sacrificed a future with a woman who was promised to him, and that your own relationship with the person you fell in love with is the reason for picking up a book on the subject.

The story of Narcissus accurately reflects the one-dimensionality of the narcissist in relationships, which we will explore in this book and which you may be able to attest to already. Anyone who has been used and abused by a narcissist (and knows it) can. An objective bystander may be able to observe it, if they are able to see through the mask. Although the narcissist can appear to be Miss Popular, with her flock of supporters in her wake, these relationships are superficial. In your own relationship, you may want intimacy, trust, and a sense of depth, but this is eternally out of your reach if you are dating or married to a narcissist. It may as well be scrawled on a billboard that the narcissist has chosen

YOU. But they have only chosen you for their use, pleasure, and entertainment, and perhaps to show off.

In the beginning of what you thought would be your own fairytale, in the early days of your relationship with your partner, you might have been giddy with the euphoria of love at first sight. She was the full package, exuding a sultry air of sex and charm that made you want to swoon, wielding her feathers like a peacock on parade (being the incorrigible exhibitionist that you fell in love with). She was charming beyond measure, whispering confessions of her undying love, swathing you in love and attention, and apparently possessing high hopes for the future of your relationship that were akin to yours. This, as you will see in the next chapter, is part of what is sometimes referred to as the 'idealization' phase. It is called this for reasons that should now be obvious, and it is the first stage, or 'honeymoon' phase that will feature again and again throughout your relationship. The fabric of a relationship with a narcissist is woven tightly around the cycle of the idealization and devaluation stages, and the never-ending push/pull or hot/cold cycle produces the same reaction in you, biochemically, as a drug addiction. The story of Narcissus reveals to us the irrepressible, lonely yearning of an addict. Although the relationship between narcissism and addiction may not be immediately apparent. More than one author has likened the "narcissistic supply" to addiction. We'll deal with the relationship between narcissism and addiction in later chapters. The nature of that relationship may not seem obvious now, but you will see that there is an element of addiction in both you and the narcissist.

It may have taken a while for you to hear the dull thud of reality to hit home. It may have taken some time for the waters surrounding your love-struck vision to become clear so that you could see that beyond the fanfare and fakery was a master of manipulation whose primary object of worship was not you, but herself. It may have taken a month, a year, or even 10, for you to realize that, like Narcissus gazing into the pool, when she gazes into your eyes, she can only see her own reflection. You realize that your own search for meaning and emotional depth in the relationship stops when she says it stops, and the intolerable superficiality finally inspires you to pick up a book on narcissism and make changes that have been a long time coming.

This introduces the complex question of the uncomfortable relationship between self-care and selfishness, and we will visit this topic again later, in the context of the spectrum of narcissistic traits and the inevitable reality that we all have them to some extent. Some semblance of self-love is necessary for the essential act of self-preservation (we will talk in chapter six about self-love as your own motivating force behind learning how to respond to a narcissist). No matter who we are and what our flaws are, any self-help book, motivational speaker, or empowerment guru will tell us that, yes, when you look in the mirror, you should see yourself as the fairest of them all. Yes, fill up your wall space with affirmations stating how handsome and admirable you are. It may sound like a cheesy cliche, but it is surely the case that on some level, the reason you are reading this book is that you do believe you are worth a bit of extra effort in the name of self-care and mental well-being. In the context of seeking to create a better life for yourself, pursuing a healthier 'normal' and, to put it bluntly, staying sane, it is necessary to cultivate a healthy sense of self worth. Having a solid self-image and self-esteem is essential to fulfilling your potential. Any psychologist would agree that this is true for everyone.

So where do we draw the line between self-love and narcissism, and what makes it ok for you to pursue self-love, but not for the person you are married to? She is also ultimately motivated by adoration of herself, despite the various masks she wears for you and others. The mirror analogy, and indeed the concept of self-love, takes a dark turn when the person looking in the mirror is either physically wired to literally not be able to empathize with others, or when her traumatic, neglected, or spoiled childhood experiences have resulted in an absence of empathy as a defense mechanism. When a narcissist looks in the proverbial mirror, their peripheral vision is impaired so that they don't see the mirror, or the rest of the background that is also reflected in the mirror, for that matter. They just see themselves. When it comes to other people who feature in the life of the narcissist, this self-focused blurring out of the background information can have a hugely detrimental effect on the relationship itself, as well as on the mental and emotional health of the other person, or people, who are involved. It takes this dangerous turn because the narcissist's actions are motivated by acquiring the 'supply.' This refers to the validation you give them, despite your lack of awareness or intention to do so, or their imagined superiority and sense of entitlement to special treatment. If the narcissist herself were an addict, she would draw her 'supply' from you in the same sense as a drug addict would need 'supply.' Other people in the narcissist's life provide an adrenaline rush, a sense of power that can only be derived by using and manipulating people like pawns for the sheer pleasure of it.

It may be hard to imagine what this looks like in practice, and my own experience testifies to the fact that it is extremely difficult to move beyond the confines of the narrative that had been created by my narcissistic spouse and recognize the true nature of what was going on in our relationship. To rephrase this in different words, it was a slow and difficult task to take ownership of how I experienced certain elements of the relationship, to trust my own perceptions. This is largely because of the various psychological techniques that form such a fundamental part of a narcissist's relationships, such as gaslighting and triangulation. If the narcissist repeatedly makes you doubt your truth by using techniques such as these, you will start doubting your beliefs, knowledge, and convictions (and ultimately yourself), and it can end up being hard to see the woods for the trees. It is hoped that, as you move through each chapter of this book, it will become easier and easier for you to realize the legitimacy of your own experiences and suspicions that something is not quite right. As you read this book, you will slowly become more familiar with the language that is used to identify the wily ways of the wayward narcissist, and thereby begin rewriting your own story. Let's start, in this chapter, by unpacking the concept of narcissism: the kinds of behavior you would expect from a narcissist, what we understand about it in layman's terms, and what it implies in a clinical context. To do this, let's take a look at some typical scenarios to see if you can identify with them.

Zack

Zack is a 31-year-old man who is married and has two kids. He has a habit of blaming other people for his own misfortune, or for things that don't go his way. A typical reaction to hearing bad news, whether it is something as small as the cashier not taking cards or something more consequential, like a flight being postponed, is to shift the blame onto others. The possibility of him having made a mistake doesn't enter his mind; it is always someone else's fault. For example, his wife describes a situation where the family wanted to go camping in summer. He was adamant about making a booking at a place that had lovely views, but when he made the booking, he was warned that the area is prone to flooding during the stormy summer season. He made the booking; he had always wanted to visit this particular venue. The camping trip had to be canceled at the last minute due to bad weather. When he heard the news, he automatically blamed the venue, launching into a narcissistic rage. He accused his wife of insisting that they go during summer, saying it was her fault they had to cancel, because they could have gone camping any time and she was the one who suggested they go during summer. Rather than accepting that he should have considered a better location to camp during that season and that he was ultimately the person who made the booking, he blamed everything and everyone else, including the weather service which had given the impression that there would be mild weather over that time. Zack refused to take

---

accountability for the part that he played in this scenario.

Nicole

Nicole is a married woman in her forties with four children who are grown up and have all left and are living independently. She lives alone with her husband of 20 years, for the first time since they have been together. Her husband has suggested they see a couple's therapist because he is struggling to navigate the relationship. He describes one incident to demonstrate her almost pathological need for control. He says that they live on the top floor in a block of apartments, so they have a good view of what is happening on the ground. One day, he noticed that there was a stray dog roaming the streets. He mentioned it in passing and picked up his phone to call the animal rescue center, but before he knew it, his wife had stopped what she was doing and was at the window. She snapped at him, instructing him to phone the animal rescue center (which he was already doing). There was no answer. Julie interrogated him, asking where he got the number from and whether he had tried another organization that might be able to help, insinuating that he was incapable of solving the problem and that he was being indecisive, as usual. She looked up other phone numbers online, sent them to him, and instructed him to call them while she went downstairs to try to catch the dog. As she went downstairs, she called people she knew in the area who might be able to help. One of them found the owner, and the owner arrived on the scene and caught the dog. Once the situation had been resolved, Julie gave a one-sided account of what happened, painting herself out to be the hero in the story, saying to her husband that he was dithering and indecisive, making jokes that suggested he was dim-witted. Her husband describes how during this incident he was feeling anxious, harassed, and insecure. This situation is a good example of the egocentric perspective that a narcissist can take in any situation without taking into account the needs of others (not to mention the possibility that they might have something valuable to offer) and the way that she needs to exert her control and dominate others in this process. The narrative Julie gave after the event is also a classic narcissist maneuver of showcasing their own contributions while omitting those of others.

Natasha

Natasha is a 32-year-old working woman with a narcissistic mother. She describes her as controlling and overpowering, and remembers feeling constantly criticized when she was growing up, like she was never good enough. Natasha is staying with her father's brother and sister-in-law, looking after their house while they go on holiday. She was asked to drive her aunty and uncle to the airport at 5:00am, and she agreed to do it, as she likes to help out and wanted to build a relationship with them. She jokingly made a comment about the early hour to her mom while they were chatting one day, assuming that they were simply chatting and that she could open up to her mother. However, later that day while Natasha was out, her mom called Natasha's aunt and told her that Natasha had said it was an inconvenience taking them. She suggested that they pay for a taxi to take them instead of Natasha, even though a taxi cost more and Natasha had already willingly agreed. They decided to take a taxi anyway. This scenario shows a number of features that you may be able to recognize. It's another example of the need for control, but also demonstrates the way in which a narcissist will create an environment of trust and use the information that you share within this environment to maintain control and, even worse, manipulate a situation for her own gain. Unfortunately, it is often the case that this means turning others against you in an effort to win support and validation for herself.

What is Narcissism?

The first port of call when discussing narcissism is to point out a few technicalities regarding the word. The word 'narcissist' may be overused and it may seem as though it has lost its meaning to some extent. With its growing presence in books and movies, as well as the narratives we use in daily discourse, we may be inclined to to accuse anyone who exhibits a semblance of self-centeredness of being a narcissist. Books tell us that narcissists are hiding everywhere, lurking where you least expect them to be, and could accost you at any point, so you'd better have your wits about you or you will be used and abused in the most heartless and damaging way.

The books that tell us these things would be right in suggesting that narcissists, as we have come to know them through the media, can't be pigeonholed to a certain profession, race, or economic status. Most narcissists are men, but beyond gender, narcissists skulk among us as businesspeople, volunteers, artists, teachers, or postal servicemen. The fact that you are reading this book indicates that you may be married to one, or you know someone who is. You wouldn't be alone in this; there is no shortage of people who leave their marriages because of narcissistic abuse.

Here is where the terms used in conversations about narcissism start to blend in to one another. Don't be fooled and think that the definitions used in everyday life are adequate to describe the pathological state of narcissism that affects people's lives and relationships in significant ways, and which often require intervention in order to diagnose, manage the effects of narcissism, and possibly even secure the safety of those intimately involved with the narcissist. Beyond the general definition of the word, let's see what the dictionary has to say about narcissism.

The Merriam-Webster Dictionary (n.d.), states that narcissism is "egoism or egocentrism" or a "love of or sexual desire of one's own body." The second quote at the beginning of this chapter also is provided as a third description of narcissism in the Merriam-Webster Dictionary (n.d.), in the context of Narcissistic Personality Disorder. This, too, is a superficial explanation; no three-line definition will ever suffice to describe the complexity that has emerged on the topic of narcissism in recent years. This being said, there is a kernel of truth in the claim that egoism does indeed play an absolutely essential role in the characterization of the narcissist—it is one of the defining features of any kind of narcissist, regardless of how extreme the narcissistic traits are. There may be some truth in the second statement provided by Merriam-Webster as well, but it is an extremely narrow way of summarizing the self-love that a narcissist embodies, which can sometimes be described as an autoerotic sexual love of oneself.

Finally, allow me to remind you of the quote by Robert Karen at the beginning of this chapter, which was included by Merriam-Webster as a description of narcissism: "One of the premier diagnoses of our times, narcissism is a reflection not only of an apparent trend in mental illness but also the strains and distortions in the lives of essentially healthy people." This quote aptly summarizes the pervasive quality of narcissism in a wide spectrum of people who display narcissistic traits, from the mildly narcissistic to the destructive whims of the pathological narcissist. Becoming familiar with and navigating this spectrum is part of the project of knowing your wife in her subtle (or not so subtle) narcissistic presence in your life. Part of the intention of this book is for you to become intimately acquainted with this spectrum and where your wife fits in: an essential step in recovering from narcissistic abuse.

Beyond these finely tuned definitions that reveal only certain aspects of narcissism, there is the context of an ever-changing body of knowledge about narcissism where one must establish a working definition. As Pincus and Roche (2011) say, "there are as many definitions for the narcissist as there are people alive." Pincus and Roche (2011) define narcissism as "one's capacity to maintain a relatively positive self-image through a variety of self-regulation, affect-regulation, and interpersonal processes, and it underlies and individuals' needs for validation and admiration, as well as the motivation to overtly and covertly seek out self-enhancement experiences from the social environment."

This is one definition of narcissism, among many. It is also a polite and objective way of summarizing the egocentric, self-centered, controlling, and manipulative ways of the narcissist. Narcissism, as you will see in the next chapter, occurs along a spectrum, with Narcissistic Personality Disorder at the far end of the spectrum (in fact, very few people have NPD). There are various types and subtypes of NPD, which will be spoken about at length later in the book. Bearing this in mind, it is important to note that all narcissists, no matter whether they are grandiose, vulnerable or malignant, somatic or cerebral, or covert or overt, have a few key identifiable traits, although they differ in the way these are expressed. Some of the traits that are present for each narcissist, regardless of the type or subtype, are an inflated sense of being better than everyone else, a pathological need for control, and having manipulative tendencies and shallow relationships with others, to name a few. These different styles of manipulation and ways of obtaining control, for example, will be dealt with in the chapter that addresses the different types and subtypes of narcissism. In this chapter we will focus on narcissism in general, and narcissism within the context of Narcissistic Personality Disorder.

So, let's elaborate upon these general traits that are common to all narcissists, regardless of the type or subtype to which they belong. Narcissists can easily shapeshift into whoever you want them to be. They wear whatever mask they need to gain support from anyone and everyone they come into contact with, who they think they can manipulate for their own gain. If you think you know a narcissist from the way they treat you when you are alone, think again as narcissists seem to become completely different people from the image they portray in the public eye. Behind closed doors they can be unceasingly critical and harsh, and yet when there are others around, they adorn a charming sweetness that could melt the hardest heart and leave the most unsuspecting people weak at the knees. They might be said to show their true colors to the people they are most intimate with, especially the grandiose narcissist. It can be a challenge to believe your own experiences when everyone else perceives them to be God's gift to the human race, who conforms to the norms of society with the enthusiasm and the air of magnificence that they believe they leave in their wake, like the hero descended from on high to rescue mankind from its own erroneous ways. The narcissist may or may not be exceptionally gifted at one thing or another, but whether they are or not is beside the point—they will have you believe they are in some way superior to others, perfect even, because that is what they believe about themselves.

Describing them as "God's gift to creation" may be a slight exaggeration, of course, but it highlights the self-absorbed nature of a narcissist and the need to blow their own trumpets to ensure that all people's eyes are on them in order to stroke their ego. They (especially the grandiose narcissists) engage in one-sided conversation that can often seem geared solely toward boastful flaunting of their accomplishments, good deeds, or martyrdom without mention of anyone else and their achievements, value, contributions, or attributes. They expect others to have a similar appreciation for their own esteemed qualities and require recognition of their almost superhuman qualities. Narcissists paint a colorful picture of their good deeds, flavoring the narrative with a not-entirely accurate depiction of the events in question that allows them to be the hero of the story (and possibly even paint others, including you, in a negative light in order to illuminate themselves in all of their glory.

Pinning down a narcissist and expressing your concern about her behavior behind closed doors is a slippery business because of this superficial front they portray to the wider public. They may appear to be friendly and charming and, indeed, appear to have all of the characteristics you might attribute to a responsible citizen who sticks to social mores like superglue. They can seem like nothing less than the pillars of society that earn the respect of everyone they encounter, and because of the constant narrative they wield in the face of unsuspecting people who engage with them, it seems believable.

This is the mask that narcissists wear. But behind closed doors, in relationships with the people they are most intimate with, they remove their masks and reveal their true identities as people who lack the capacity for empathy and have a larger-than-life ego that takes on grandiose proportions and an inflated sense of entitlement that is allowed full expression with loved ones. While the public act may seem convincing, it is a guise used for the narcissist's own benefit and is by no means genuine, although many an innocent onlooker has been fooled by his or her beguiling ways. It is only after weeks or even months of use that the narcissist starts to lose interest in people who were once very valuable to him or her and discards them without so much as a "thank you."

It was mentioned earlier that finding validation for the challenges you face as the husband of a narcissist can be an uphill battle, and that building a support system from your circle of friends and family can be a struggle. This is in no small way due to the fact that the narcissist presents herself as glibly and charmingly as the feminine equivalent of the proverbial knight in shining armor who wins people over with a syrupy compliment or what is seen as an act of kindness.

Aside from the superficial, false front that is presented to the world, there are a host of other qualities that are associated with narcissism. One of the defining characteristics of all narcissists is their unsurpassed lack of empathy, a complete obliviousness to other people's emotions, and an inability to recognize their needs. Whether you are a friend, someone she encounters at a party, or her partner, you (as a person) are a means to an end for a narcissist, an object to be used for her own gain. She expects others to do her bidding and can't understand it if they don't. There is a genuine expectation that she deserves to be treated as special, and that her superiority should be likewise comprehended by all other people who have a heartbeat. While she may appear to be courteous and generous, this is a front that is motivated by her own needs and desires rather than heartfelt empathy or compassion. Most if not all relationships that a narcissist has are transactional and superficial; she lacks the ability to have meaningful connections with people.

Besides the analogy of the mirror that features often in the vocabulary of people talking about narcissists, the metaphor of the mask is often used in relevant literature to highlight the discrepancy between the narcissist's true self and the false self that he or she wields to the public, like a salesman exhibiting his finest wares before a crowd of interested shoppers. It also can refer to the number of different faces that the narcissist can adopt in adapting to different people and contexts, like a chameleon, to make them likeable, attractive, and worth investing time and energy into anyone and everyone. The narcissist needs to adorn these masks, and in this way be super-flexible in the way he or she embodies different identities, to summon validation, support, and attention from others. The group of people that ends up trailing along in the narcissist's wake is an essential resource for the narcissist, whether they know it or not (and usually they don't, in the beginning phases of their relationship anyway).

Behary (2013) describes four primary masks that the narcissist adopts. Although in this book, we will be using the analogy of the mask to make a contrast between the charming, sweet persona that dominates social situations and the rather cruel person who emerges once the audience has dissipated, we will use these four different personas described by Behary to highlight key characteristics that we can come to recognize in the narcissist. These four 'masks' explained here allow us to recognize when typical narcissistic scenarios arise, and respond appropriately.

First off is "the show off" (Behary, 2013). However unintentional it may be, the version of the narcissist that flaunts his or her attributes, skills, achievements, and accomplishments as if she is competing for Miss World is using you to get a sense of appreciation, attention and validation that can't be derived internally (Behary, 2013). Instead of being honest about the contributions of others, she exaggerates the role that she has played, and rather than finding value and being satisfied with the integrity that arises from an inner recognition of the good that she has done, she relies on your approval (Behary, 2013).

The second mask is that of the 'bully' (Behary, 2013). It's a mask because it hides a fragile sense of self and a deep-seated district of others that stems from past experiences (Behary, 2013). The sense of power he derives from sending you an unceasing onslaught of criticisms, insults, and questions that whittle your own sense of self down to a husk compensates for his lack thereof (Behary, 2013). The ways that the narcissist can bully you take a wide range of forms. In the case of the grandiose narcissist, it can take the form of outright insults, while the vulnerable narcissist will insinuate things in a passive-aggressive way without directly saying them.

When the narcissist dons the mask of what Behary (2013) calls "the entitled one," she waltzes into the scene expecting her wants and needs to be met, no matter what the sacrifice by others. If she doesn't get her heart's desires, she can't understand why. She believes she can act however she wants regardless of consequences, that she is superior to everyone else, and that she therefore deserves special treatment. She doesn't care how this affects people as she is unable to focus on their needs or locate herself within the context of people who may have different opinions about her place on the imaginary hierarchy she has in her mind. She sees herself placed in prime position on the top tier, always wielding the gold medal no matter the circumstances, who gets injured along the way, or the degree of contributions that were made by others.

Finally, the "addictive self-soother" will stop at nothing to displace her true feelings of loneliness and shame behind whatever selfish distraction she can find (Behary, 2013). This could mean shopping, drinking, watching TV, or launching into a characteristic monologue with you that is completely closed off to any input from your side, no matter how endearing or loving it is. The narcissist masks pain even from herself, and can use a variety of methods to restore a sense of comfort to herself, despite the fact that it may be in the form of a destructive habit.

This is just a brief account of the various characteristics of narcissists, and it may still be hard to judge from this introductory text to what extent your wife is, in fact, a narcissist. As you proceed through this book, it will get easier to judge. Chapter five will provide a summary and concise checklist that can help you to clarify this and whether your wife might even qualify as abusive.

Physical abuse is far easier to spot than emotional or verbal abuse. It can be a constant source of pain, an incessant whittling away of your confidence and self-esteem and an assault to your energy and identity. It takes a heightened awareness to notice the subtle forms of abuse that pervasive sarcasm, cutting comments, and unnecessary jibes can take. There doesn't need to be a dramatic event for emotional abuse to be taking place. It's in the small things—the tone of voice or the gestures that are used can cut the deepest, especially when they are done on a repetitive basis. The ins and outs of narcissistic abuse will be discussed further in chapter five.

Suffice it to say, for now, that you know you are in the relentless clutches of a narcissist if you feel like you have to keep earning your place in the relationship. Being in the merciless presence of a narcissist can be likened to a puppy strung along on a lead. The narcissist gets a kick out of keeping you on a string, making you practically beg for forgiveness for all your so-called heinous misdeeds that make you feel like filth, even though you have done nothing wrong. The narcissist has a working knowledge of the vulnerable human mind and will stop at nothing to use this knowledge merely for a sense of enjoyment at your suffering. One moment she will be showering you with compliments, boosting your confidence, and showing her appreciation of you, and in the next instant, she will be giving you the cold shoulder or stone-walling you into submission. This cyclical manipulation that ultimately forms the basis of an addiction will be discussed here.

This is akin to a reward/punishment system that is essentially being used to keep you begging for more (Arabi, 2016). No matter how badly you are being treated, you are so focused on receiving the next reward that you don't notice and are oblivious to the fact that the reward has been carefully and artfully timed to ensure you are teetering on the edge of desperation, when the heroine sweeps back into the story to rescue you from your lonely fate. Intermittent rewards (e.g. compliments or presents) are given occasionally for the desired behavior, rather than being given consistently for the behavior that is required from you (Arabi, 2016).

Being Victim to Narcissism as an Addiction

Addiction can be defined in different ways, and one of the ways is to say that it is a biochemical process that involves the release of certain chemicals in your body—the same chemicals that are involved in addiction to drugs, which include oxytocin, dopamine, adrenaline and cortisol (Arabi, 2016). Oxytocin is a hormone that creates feelings of trust, comfort, and attachment (Arabi, 2016). It has a strong presence during the honeymoon, or idealization, phase of a relationship (as one phase in the narcissistic relationship, which we will discuss later along with the other phases in the abuse cycle). This is especially so in a relationship with a narcissist and the rain of affection that tends to ooze from narcissists early on in a relationship. In the extreme case of the latter, though, oxytocin will continue to be produced throughout the relationship as you are buffeted from the euphoria of being worshipped like you are a deity, to the doldrums of despair during the devaluation phase. This is the dramatic emotional landscape that keeps you coming back for more despite abuse, that eventually leads you to addiction to the chaos, and closer and closer to a dissolution of your sense of self-worth and your sense of self. This feeling can be amplified through intercourse, further deepening our trust through increased levels of oxytocin that occur during the sexual act (Arabi, 2016).

The second chemical that plays an important role here is dopamine, which is most often associated with addiction to cocaine (Arabi, 2016). It comes down, with dopamine, to the love-hate relationship we have with our narcissistic partners and our turbulent emotional experiences with them—the push/pull feeling that you get when you think about her—being in love with her, but also knowing that she makes you suffer (Arabi, 2016). Dopamine responds well to the intermittent reinforcement that you know so well, the inconsistent supply of reward in the form of canoodling, sex, gifts...whatever makes you happy, and whatever makes you want more of it (Arabi, 2016). A cognitive dissonance arises in our minds—a desperate clinging onto the idea of the person we thought we knew in the face of incomprehensible pain that is caused by the narcissist's alter ego, or what we might call the "true self" (Arabi, 2016). The memory of the abuse sparks a hypervigilance, and the memory of highly pleasurable experiences is a recipe for disaster (Arabi, 2016).

Cortisol is yet another hormone that is released when you are stressed, which does not work in your favor if you want to heal from traumatic experiences with narcissists (Arabi, 2016). It's a stress hormone that comes from your adrenal glands as you barely hang on to the emotional rollercoaster involved in life with a narcissist. It is secreted as a response to fear, and contributes (along with oxytocin) toward the consolidation of memories that involve fear (Arabi, 2016). It is secreted when you experience new traumatic events, as well as when you remember things that made you afraid in the past, thus embedding trauma deeply into the fabric of your physical being, making it harder to move on (Arabi, 2016).

Adrenaline is another relevant hormone that is related to feelings of love, as well as fear (Arabi, 2016). When two people who love each other share an intense experience, or one that is particularly fearful, they tend to be more closely bound together than if they hadn't; this is due to adrenaline and dopamine (Arabi, 2016). You become more closely bonded through traumatic experiences with someone—this applies to the fear that you feel in a narcissistic relationship when you wonder what your wife has in store for you next. Adrenaline also acts as an antidepressant, which in turn leads to the secretion of dopamine in situations when you are afraid or anxious (Arabi, 2016).

Serotonin is also involved here, and is involved in the regulation of moods (Arabi, 2016). Having feelings of being in love with someone leads to a drop in serotonin levels, which in turn affects an individual's sexual behavior, making them more likely to engage in sexual activity (Arabi, 2016). Sexual activity stimulates the release of oxytocin and dopamine, which, as we have seen, is part of the addictive cycle (Arabi, 2016). And so the cycle continues.

All of this culminates in what Arabi (2016) and other writers call "trauma bonding"—an attachment that we develop to people who do us harm, as a result of the abuse that we endure with them. At best, trauma bonding can lead to unhealthy attachment to a destructive situation and toxic person; at worst, you start to defend your abuser and lose your own identity in the process.

As you can see, being stuck in a relationship with a narcissist is not as simple as it looks. Not only is there an endless series of psychological factors involved in keeping people trapped in the torment of being in a relationship with a narcissist, but the patterns within the relationship cause a physical reaction that forms the basis of an addiction. This is why it can be so hard to keep the "no contact" contract with yourself (described in chapter six), despite your best intentions. Staying away from your partner is literally equivalent to trying to stop taking drugs, and like a drug addict, you may experience withdrawal when you terminate the relationship with your spouse and cease to make contact (Arabi, 2016). On a physical level, this promotes the release of the hormone oxytocin in your body, which stimulates feelings of attachment and trust (Arabi, 2016). This chemical is involved in addictive patterns. So, what is happening here is that you are essentially addicted to the relationship. Living in an environment with the perpetual threat of abuse hanging over you like the dense, heavy air before a summer storm is an environment in which you are constantly in survival mode, fighting for your sanity, treading the turbulent waters until you are giving the sweet relief of a reward. This is why victims stay in abusive relationships. This is why you may find it hard to take the "no contact approach." The problem is that there is no rehabilitation center for recovering narcissists. However, there is hope.

Chapter six will give you some ideas about how you can stimulate the release of the chemicals mentioned above without having anything to do with your wife. But, before we discuss the various measures you can take to protect yourself against a narcissist in chapters five and six, we will further explore the different types and subtypes of narcissism, as well as the current theories that might explain the possible causes behind the development of narcissistic features. For now, let us define Narcissistic Personality Disorder and compare it with milder versions of narcissism.

Narcissistic Personality Disorder

We have indicated in this chapter that narcissistic traits lurk in all of us, and that narcissistic traits feature on a spectrum that ranges in extremity of these traits. At the furthest end of the NPI (a scale that is used for measuring narcissism, which will be discussed in more detail later in this book) is Narcissistic Personality Disorder (NPD). NPD is becoming an increasingly popular topic of discussion in the field of psychology and psychiatry and is likewise entering into the dialogue of more and more laypeople, with more people becoming aware of individuals who display the traits of the narcissist anywhere from workplaces to families and circle of friends, for example.

Narcissistic Personality Disorder is a personality disorder that features in the Diagnostic and Statistical Manual of Psychiatry. People who can be said to have this condition exhibit a lack of empathy and a sense of grandiosity in at least five of nine possible indicators, including arrogance, self-importance, envy and the pervasive tendency to use other people for their own gain without recognizing the needs of others (Diagnostic and Statistical Manual of Psychiatry, 2013).

We have discussed the general traits of narcissists, the characteristics that all narcissists have in common. But we can go even deeper than that and differentiate between the different types and subtypes of narcissism that are labeled according to certain 'symptoms' or, to put it more accurately, methods by which they retain control over and manipulate others.

Types of narcissist include the classic narcissist, the vulnerable narcissist, and the malignant narcissist, all noticeable for their extreme lack of empathy and sense of superiority, but who differ in terms of how they go about expressing this through their behavior (DavidJohn, 2018). The classic narcissist is the typical narcissist we all know and love to hate. With an inflated sense of superiority and desperation to be in the spotlight, the classic narcissist can't bear the thought of others getting the attention that they rightfully deserve and will stop at nothing to prevent that from happening. They are sometimes labeled as 'exhibitionist' or 'high-functioning' narcissists (DavidJohn, 2018). Vulnerable narcissists (also otherwise known as "compensatory narcissists," "closet narcissists," or "fragile narcissists") have an equally inflated ego, but don't enjoy being in the limelight (DavidJohn, 2018). On the contrary, they gain people's attention by adopting the role of the victim that elicits pity from people, or they find validation in people's appreciation by being overly generous (DavidJohn, 2018). The third type, malignant narcissism, is when the person exhibits antisocial or sadistic tendencies that could be likened to those of the sociopath or psychopath (DavidJohn, 2018). These traits might be displayed in the form of highly manipulative, controlling behavior. In the wake of actions that might cause harm to others, they feel no remorse and may even revel in the suffering of others (DavidJohn, 2018).

On top of this, professionals also make a distinction between covert and overt narcissists, and cerebral and somatic narcissists. Let's start with the first. All narcissists achieve their goals in either a covert or an overt way. Classic narcissists tend toward being more overt. This means that they will get what they want in an open, non-surreptitious way that is unashamedly unapologetic (DavidJohn, 2018). The more covertly inclined specimens (usually vulnerable narcissists) are more secretive and cunning about achieving what they want (DavidJohn, 2018). Instead of nonchalantly going about their in-your-face tactics, they will control and manipulate the situation in the background. Malignant narcissists can be either one of the two (DavidJohn, 2018).

Another way of grouping narcissists into subtypes is to distinguish between somatic and cerebral. This categorization essentially expresses the object toward which the narcissist focuses his or her obsession with self (Vaknin, 2014). The somatic narcissist is obsessed with his or her body—they can't help but be overzealous about keeping in shape and admiring and working on their physical appearance. Cerebral narcissists regard their intelligence and general omniscience to be traits that set them worlds apart from the average person, and indeed all other people!

As to whether narcissists are aware of their self-centeredness, there is no answer that can be applied universally for all narcissists in the same way that generalizations don't apply to all human beings. According to an article on Psychology Today, most narcissists do admit to being self-centered (Narcissism, n.d.). The author of that article also suggests that the easiest way to find out whether they are able to identify narcissistic qualities in themselves is, quite simply, to ask them (Narcissism, n.d.).

Fair enough. However, taking into account what we already know about narcissists and the kinds of self-fulfilling environments they tend to conjure up at your expense, it is up to you whether it is worth bringing it up. Ensure that you do so in a safe environment—as you will see (or maybe you know already from your experience with your spouse), catching her at the wrong time could cause a verbal mudslinging in your general direction. In saying this, though, it is a rare event for a narcissist to attend therapy. This is because a narcissist who attends counseling has probably been encouraged to go by relatives who are desperate for change. There is no reason for her to go to therapy because she is the one benefiting most from her narcissistic behavior, and it is highly unlikely that she will go for your or anyone else's sake. The vulnerable narcissist may be an exception here—they more easily recognize that something is awry and are often willing to change. In either case, though, meaningful and lasting change is pretty much unattainable.

And so the inevitable question that arises here is whether or not your partner can change. Tony Sayers, author of *Energy Vampires: How to Protect Yourself From Toxic People with Narcissistic Tendencies* (2018), seems to think not. The major qualities of character that define the narcissist, like perpetually thinking they are better than everyone else, makes them highly unlikely to believe you if you point out their flaws, no matter how tactful you try to be about it (Sayers, 2018). Plus, it wouldn't be in a narcissist's interest to seek help, as they are the ones who derive the most amount of gain from their disorder!

The question of *why* mental disorder occurs, and indeed why it often seems like prevalence is on the rise, is a major topic of research in psychology, and has been for as long as it has existed. This particular topic of study is called etiology; it looks at the causes behind mental disorders (or diseases in medicine). Narcissism is not excluded as a subject of etiological study, but it is less researched than disorders like depression and anxiety. Although much of the emphasis was put on the role of parenting when people first started theorizing about it, there is a general movement toward an understanding of the development of narcissism as an interplay between brain structure, genetics, and upbringing. The exact nature of the relationship between these three factors is not quite clear, but this is the general direction that current theory is taking. We will explore the dance that these elements have with one another in chapter four. For now, we will proceed to unpack the concept of Narcissistic Personality Disorder as a clinical mental disorder and explore the meaning of narcissistic abuse and what it might look like.

Chapter 2:

Narcissism Under the

Microscope

In the last chapter, we took a look in the mirror to see what kind of reflection it might reveal of the narcissist, and we learned that narcissism is not all that it seems. While we may be inclined to think that the definition of narcissism is as simple as what you might find in a dictionary, it is not. We have learned that we all have narcissistic traits, and that some of us teeter closer to the pathological disorder known as Narcissistic Personality Disorder. When we look in our own mirrors of reflection, we might find traces of narcissism, but these can be harmless, and even part of self-preservation. However, having extreme, clinically diagnosable levels of narcissism can have debilitating effects on those closest to the narcissist (even though technically, it may not affect them in any adverse way).

General narcissism aside, we will now adopt a stronger lens to examine in greater detail the ins and outs of Narcissistic Personality Disorder in particular, and we will do it first by discussing the ways in which narcissism can be measured, and how NPD can be diagnosed, when compared with less extreme forms of narcissism. The goal of this chapter is to help you to gain a more intimate understanding of it as a mental disorder, as you get up close and personal with the true self of your spouse, beyond the mask she chooses to show the public. It will also help you to get a broader perspective of the circumstances you find yourself in, take your situation less personally and therefore be less reactive when your wife triggers you in the future. We will also lay out the kinds of techniques that people with NPD employ to master you and anyone who dares step in her path (but mainly you).

Measuring Narcissism

We all know that person who manipulates people by being two-faced, and who likes to bask in the limelight and soak up all the attention that onlookers are willing to provide. We may be one of them, if we are honest with ourselves. But what differentiates the narcissist from your everyday gossip-monger who can't get enough of the juicy stuff? Or the colleague in the cubicle next door who likes to rant on and on about his incomparable efficiency at work? Narcissism is measured on a scale called the Narcissistic Personality Inventory (NPI), which was the brainchild of Robert Raskin and Calvin Hall in 1979 (Webber, 2016). We all fit in there somewhere.

The NPI, according to Webber (2016), is a test that is completed by the person who is being tested. They are given a set of questions, with two possible answers. The answers measure levels of assertiveness, the extent to which they are open to adopt a leadership role, modesty and their level of eagerness to manipulate other people (Webber, 2016). This test is useful in the sense that it can provide an indication of where a person features on a spectrum of Narcissistic Traits, where most people score in the mid-teens (Webber, 2016). However, although it can give a measure of extreme narcissism, it can't be used to diagnose Narcissistic Personality Disorder (Webber, 2016). For this, a professional in the field of mental health is required, and one of the qualifying criteria for a diagnosis is that their narcissistic traits impede their day-to-day functioning in some way that could be related to tension in relationships resulting from lack of empathy (Webber, 2016). What would differentiate an extreme narcissist from someone with NPD is that, in the case of the latter, the defense mechanisms (that appear as the symptoms that have been previously discussed), are always operational.

Narcissistic Personality Disorder

So, while we might all have whispers of the narcissist within our minds, and evidence in our behavior, nothing quite beats being diagnosed as having Narcissistic Personality Disorder, as you will know if you live with someone who has this disorder. We have concluded that the NPI does not suffice to measure NPD as a disorder. Here are the conditions that classify the symptoms of this disorder, as it is described in the DSM-5 (2013). Narcissistic Personality Disorder necessarily includes five or more of the following symptoms:

1. Has a grandiose sense of self importance (exaggerates achievements and talents, expects to be recognized as superior without commensurate achievements)
2. Is preoccupied with fantasies of unlimited success, power, brilliance, beauty or ideal love
3. believes he or she is "special" or unique and can only be understood by, or associate with, other special or high-status people (or institutions)
4. Requires excessive admiration
5. Has a sense of entitlement (i.e. unreasonable expectations of especially favorable treatment or automatic compliance with his or her expectations)
6. Is interpersonally exploitative (i.e. takes advantage of others to achieve his or her own ends)
7. Lacks empathy: is unwilling to recognize or identify with the feelings or needs of others
8. Is often envious of others or believes that others are envious of him or her
9. Shows arrogant or haughty behaviors or attitudes

Above is the clinical definition of NPD that is used by psychiatrists to diagnose and treat personality disorders. Another characteristic of this disorder is that the symptoms, as they are described above, occur repetitively, and that they usually appear by the time the individual reaches adulthood (DSM-5, 2013). To people who encounter the narcissist in everyday life, he or she can appear vain and boastful. Looking a little deeper into the demanding tendency to appeal to people for their praise, you can see an insecurity and a need for validation. Eruptions of anger are not uncommon when narcissists don't get their way, as they expect the world to bend and sway to their every need as it orbits around them. Their infallible sense of superiority over others gives them a sense of confidence with which they walk through the world and bestow their talents, skills and generosity among who they consider their unfortunate inferiors, and they expect to be recognized as such, to be seen gracing the lives of ordinary people with their superior presence. When it comes to expressing their high opinion of themselves, they don't hold back. Despite being more than willing to give a generous account of their own accomplishments, their willingness to paint others in a positive light is negligible, bordering on non-existent. Although they value the input of others when it comes to stroking their ego and validating their high self-esteem, they are proportionally resistant when it comes to hearing negative opinions about them from others. It should come as no surprise that relationships that narcissists are in are often perceived to be unfulfilling and empty.

What to Expect From a Narcissist

On top of the various qualities of character that you might expect from a narcissist, which you have become familiar with from preceding discussions, there are also a number of classically narcissistic maneuvers that the narcissist attempts to provoke and manipulate you. Given the fact that dialogue surrounding the topic of narcissism is on the increase, there is a growing awareness and vocabulary that aid conversation on the topic. There are a number of classic tricks that the narcissist is notorious for using, behaviorally speaking. These will be described here, and you will find that the terms used are commonly used vocabulary to anyone who is in active dialogue about this topic. The purpose of elaborating upon them here is to help you identify when they are happening in your own life, so that you will be more prepared. The situations described above demonstrate specific, and well-documented tactics that are cunningly fashioned by the narcissist to derive 'supply' from you. These techniques are described by Arabi (2016) as follows:

1. Triangulation

2. Gaslighting

3. Smear Campaigns

4. Love-bombing

Triangulation is a special kind of psychological warfare tactic that is used to control your emotions, usually by inciting a sense of jealousy or insecurity in the victim. This is achieved by bringing a third person into the picture, either through conversation, physical presence or comments on social media with the intention of distracting you from the issues or actions in your relationship that are cause for concern (Arabi, 2016). Essentially, triangulation is when the narcissist tries to control people who are part of a group of three, to gain some advantage. For example, she may mention how an ex-lover has initiated contact now that he has returned from his travels. Or, she may confide in you, enticing you to share your innermost feelings toward the other person and then go behind your back, and break that trust by sharing what you told her with the other person. As a third example, your wife might use you and another person to launch herself into a position in which you and the other person start to compete with each other to gain the approval or acceptance from your wife. Note that triangulation can occur in any relationship, not just with a narcissist, but it is a very common strategy that is used often by the narcissist to keep you begging for her, and deriving supply from you, and others, in whatever way she can.

Michelle and John

Michelle and John are both in their mid-twenties, and have been in a relationship for four years. A new neighbor called Jill has moved in recently and now lives across the road. Michelle and John have met her, and got on very well with one another. They exchanged numbers. John seems to like Jill, and often when Michelle gets home from work, she notices that John is across the road talking to her.

John idealizes Jill in front of Michelle, talking at length about how great she is and painting her out to be perfect. Sometimes John brings up in conversation how great Jill is, and lists in details all the things that he likes about her.

Michelle ends up comparing herself to Jill, to the extent that she is jealous of her and the way she is loved by John. She feels as though she is lacking in some way and doesn't live up to John's standards, doesn't deserve

---

him and that she needs to do better to earn his love.

John uses Michelle as a lever to catapult himself to an unattainable position, to keep Michelle feeding his supply, making him the ever-increasing object of her attention. He may even use his relationship with Jill, and Michelle's reaction to it, against Michelle by accusing her, for example, of being oversensitive.

Gaslighting is a technique that can be said to be one of the primary techniques and strategies a narcissist used to invalidate you, and your attempts to hold them accountable for their unacceptable behavior (Arabi, 2016). We suggested earlier that it is sometimes difficult for the victim of narcissistic abuse to seek help precisely because they have nobody to verify how they are feeling. In no case is this more obvious than when the narcissist dodges all responsibility for making you feel the way you do. While this may seem like an innocent statement that may appear in any argument, the fact is that narcissists often hone in on those who are typically quite sensitive in order to get their supply. Other criticisms might also be launched in your direction, that remove accountability from the actions of the narcissist. The question here is not whether there may be truth to what the narcissist is saying to you; it is whether she can listen to what you are saying, reflect upon it and decide whether, for the sake of your relationship, she can admit to having done something wrong. It is most often the case that the narcissist won't want to do this, in the interest of a healthy, mutually respectful relationship. At the end of it, the repetition of the verbal bludgeoning by the narcissistic abuser can literally make the victim mistrust his own perception.

To provide another example of gaslighting, when you calmly call her out for behavior that seems unacceptable, for example, she will most likely overreact, calling you over-sensitive. She might bombard you with insults and fall into a narcissistic rage. Instead of listening to your perspective, reflecting upon it and disagreeing, the narcissist responds explosively, in an emotionally reactive way and immature way that leaves no space for the possibility that the criticism against them could be valid.

This pattern of gaslighting is not just used when you express your concern for their behavior. The narcissist has a knack for projecting his or her flaws upon you, thereby feigning responsibility and making you the perpetual bad guy. Instead of recognizing that they are manipulative or possessive, for example, they will accuse you of being manipulative or possessive.

Josephine and Michael

Michael and Josephine are in their fifties, and came to therapy at Josephines request, after she got the opinion of a concerned friend who was worried about how confused and disorientated Josephine seemed to be sometimes, and who also noticed that Josephine was very quiet when Michael was around. Michael was attending therapy Josephine decided to see a counselor because of the advice of her friend, and she did admit that sometimes she felt like she was losing her mind. After a couple of sessions, Josephine happened to mention a comment that Michael had made one day that triggered her into thinking that she was going mad. Reluctant at first, Josephine started giving accounts of

---

things that Michael does that makes her doubt herself and feel like she is going crazy. She mentioned one event As therapy continued, Josephine came to realize the extent to which Michael did make her doubt herself. this came across in many different ways: sometimes he would say things and then pretend that he didn't, he made her believe that she had done something that she didn't remember doing, or when she spoke out against him, he would say that he was noticing how she wasn't acting herself lately and asked her if she was ok and if she needed to see a therapist. He would use her vulnerabilities and insecurities and weaknesses in the past as weapons to remind her that she is unstable, and largely to blame when she had a complaint to make about his behavior, or when things went wrong. For example, she had experienced anxiety a couple of years back, and had seen a therapist then. When she called him out for being overly aggressive with her, he suggested that she was having an "episode" and should think about returning to therapy. Josephine realized that he was constantly doing things like this and making subtle hints and comments alluding to the idea that she was to blame, and that this ultimately formed an undertone for much of their interactions.

Smear campaigns are exactly what they promise to be: an attempt by the narcissist to make you look bad, possibly in the wake of your attempt to speak out against them (Arabi, 2016). They may lie about you, twisting the truth, or they might use information you've shared with them against you. They could paint you out to be crazy or oversensitive. they might do this for a number of reasons. Speaking your truth under the watchful eye of the harem can often prove to be a pointless task, as your complaints easily fall on deaf ears when you are up against the charm, charisma and generosity of the fake persona the narcissist adopts around others. Smear campaigns can happen while you are still in a relationship, but they can happen once you have left as well.

Bernadette and Lincoln

Bernadette and Lincoln's are in their 14th year of marriage.

However, it wasn't long after the initial honeymoon phase of their relationship that Bernadette started giving Lincoln the cold shoulder for no apparent reason, and started saying things about him behind his back to his family and friends. As time wore on, Lincoln began to feel more and more desperate to please Bernadette as he felt like he was never doing anything right, no matter how hard he tried. She kept comparing him to her other friends, which made him feel even worse. He found that he often had to explain his actions to her, until eventually he gave up trying to do things that he enjoyed, because it was simply easier than having to account for his actions all the time. He started to doubt his every choice.

One day, while Bernadette was out, he shared his troubles with a friend who noticed that he was becoming more and more reserved and submissive toward her. He decided to take action and confront her about it, but she accused him of taking things too personally all the time, and said it was his fault that he felt that way, bringing up all the mistakes he had made in the past that proved he took things too personally

---

and was too sensitive.

He decided to leave, and cut all ties with her, and a smear campaign started to snowball against him at a rapid pace. He learned that his wife was spreading rumors about him that weren't true among his family, friends and even some of his customers. She tried to convince the court that he was abusing his children, and that is why she told him to leave. Bernadette took every opportunity to make him look bad, out of spite and the desire to punish him and see him suffer for daring to stand up to her and leave.

The anecdotes described earlier describe a defining characteristic of many narcissists, that is, the need for control. This trait can manifest in various forms. Do you recall the behavior of your partner in the early phases of your relationship? If so, you may recall an exaggerated need to adorn you with compliments or vows of undying love at a premature point in the relationship, or the expression of a need to be spending time with you more often than what is considered healthy or normal. Love-bombing is another feature that may define a person's relationship with a narcissist (Arabi, 2016). It refers to exactly what its name implies: being bombarded by expressions of love and an overstepping of boundaries. When you are in a phase of love-bombing, you will be made to feel special and loved, and perhaps even as though you have met the woman of your dreams. She may claim to have the same hobbies, interests and passions as you, but this is just a farce to build rapport with you and ultimately win you over (Arabi, 2016). Despite the fact that the relationship is in its early phases, she will try her best to create an atmosphere of trust so that you pour your heart out to her. This is the beginning of the love hormones in your body to start working and become associated with such experiences. However, the sad reality is that even at this stage of the relationship she is manipulating you, although in your eyes she won't be, because you are lovestruck and you are almost at the point of thinking she is "the one."

Robin and Andrew

These two lovebirds met seven years ago. To outsiders, they seemed the perfect match. When they met, it was love at first sight. They had a lot in common, Robin knew when they were on their first date that Andrew would be the man she would marry. They would sometimes finish each other's sentences, they were forever canoodling and gazing into each other's eyes, whispering sweet nothings. Robin and Andrew were always together and Robin kept telling all of her friends how she loved spending time with him, how he spoiled her often with flowers and chocolates, and how great he was in the bedroom. She described her experience to friends as though she was in a "whirlwind of romance," and how she thought she had met "the one" from day one. Nobody was surprised when three months after they met, they were engaged.

When she was at therapy, Robin sometimes fondly remembered the first few months of the relationship, and the happy memories they had. She describes how nice Andrew could be sometimes, even throughout the relationship he had moments where they were fine and he took her back to that feeling where she felt so loved and appreciated, by telling her how great she was, and

---

making a point of taking some time out of his busy schedule especially to treat her to dinner or take her to a movie. especially after they had a fight or she messed up in some way. She said that "he could be such a softy" when he wanted to, and when he showed this side of himself she believed that everything was going to be ok. She went on to say that these moments didn't last for long, and that it didn't take much to trigger him into becoming his old self again. She wanted his soft side to last forever and her heart sank when their random date nights came to an end.

Though you quickly disembark from cloud nine to the harsh truth that you have been played like a fool, love-bombing will become a feature of your relationship that will pop up intermittently for months or years to come. It is an integral part of the cyclical movement from adoration to devaluation. More on this in the next section.

It goes without saying that the qualities described above don't necessarily make your spouse a narcissist—not only do other mental disorders exist that could explain such type of behavior, but if it this type of behavior doesn't occur on a continued basis, then it technically doesn't qualify as Narcissistic Personality Disorder.

The Cycle of Narcissistic Abuse

In the previous chapter, you became vaguely acquainted with the terms "idealization" and "devaluation" as parts of the life-cycle of a typical relationship with a narcissist. These can be part of an ongoing movement involving as many as five different phases: idealization, devaluation, discarding, destroying, and hoovering (Arabi, 2016).

We saw that the relationship usually begins with an idealization phase that surpasses the hesitant, coy beginnings of most normal relationships, in the sense that it is dominated by overzealous attempts to make you feel special and adored, and the need to control and an unhealthy need to be in contact with you constantly form an inescapable part of this reality (Arabi, 2016). The narcissist will try anything to earn your trust, and will entrust their deepest, darkest secrets to you and make you feel like you can do the same. This is an essential part of the narcissist's plan to win your trust, and to form the bonds that will define the imbalanced nature of your relationship with your partner, and your role in it (Arabi, 2016). Flattery is the name of the game, and manipulation tactics start to enter the scene here—pretty believable ones at that. Along with smothering you with love, the narcissist will pretend they have more in common with you than they actually do, to try to win you over (Arabi, 2016). At this point in the relationship, she will be who you want her to be. You might receive an endless supply of messages asking what you are doing, or asking you out or who you are with. This can be flattering and can indeed make you feel special, and that kind of treatment is hard to argue with, when you think you have stumbled upon the love of your life. However, it is an important sign that your potential suitor is possessive and lacks boundaries.

You may be able to recognize the idealization phase that roped you into the relationship in the first place, but it doesn't only happen when you first meet someone. The abuse starts within the idealization phase, seeping in every now and then without you realizing it, like poison taking hold of an unsuspecting victim. This starts to acclimatize you to the abuse, to start making you dependent on the reward that happens in the form of the way that she, in the wake of the hurtful acts that occur during the devaluation phase, adopts the mask of lover and friend and caring partner (Arabi, 2016). This act may make you feel appreciated, but it really just seeks to reinforce your codependency (Arabi, 2016). You should be familiar with one version of the idealization phase, when the allure of "love-bombing" had its hold over you and fooled you into believing that she was "the one" and marrying her.

Devaluation can take many forms—it is designed to make you feel completely worthless and insecure (Arabi, 2016). During this phase, your confidence will take a knock due to the host of nasty strategies discussed in the previous chapter, that the narcissist will use to manipulate you, control you and watch you squirm. The particular method of manipulation depends on what type of narcissist he or she is. The grandiose narcissist will, for example, occupy the limelight in no uncertain terms to garner attention from innocent bystanders, while the vulnerable narcissist will adopt a full-on victim status to make them feel loved, special and deserving of attention. One of the scariest things that can happen during the devaluation phase is that the narcissist makes you believe that everything is your fault, that she is, if anything, the victim in the story (Arabi, 2016). This happens because your sense of self-worth has been sanded down to nothing through the constant barrage of snarky, sarcastic remarks, insinuations, criticisms and insults. Both your strengths and your weakness will be used against you, so that you always feel like you are never good enough no matter what you do right (Arabi, 2016). This is because you have become reliant upon the idealization phase, dependent upon validation from your partner and need her approval to feel worthy. You can try to say something about how you feel to your spouse, or tell others about it, but the narcissist will minimize their behavior (Arabi, 2016). Ultimately you will be the one who is accused of being crazy and unreasonable, and this will make you doubt yourself even further.

Next on the agenda is the "discard" phase. Like a used tea bag, you will be heartlessly thrown aside now that you are no longer providing the narcissist with supply. In the cat-and-mouse game of your relationship, you have become the injured mouse and are no longer worth teasing as you don't provide the reaction the narcissist seeks, the rush of adrenaline that you invoke every time your rise to the challenge (Arabi, 2016), because after the endless idealization-devaluation cycle you are tired, drained and no longer have the energy to take the bait like you did in the beginning. The narcissist has decided that it is time for a new victim, a fresh supply.

We all know that being ruthlessly discarded, often without warning, can be painful enough. But being discarded from a relationship with a narcissist can take an unnecessarily painful guide, if the narcissist decides she wants to take a final stab (Arabi, 2016). She will use the final opportunity to make you feel like garbage to its fullest potential, split up with you without communicating her intention, and may even use techniques like gaslighting and triangulation to make you look like a fool and add fuel to the flame of your suffering (Arabi, 2016). The moment, for them, is ripe for publicly humiliating you, or worse. And then, you will probably find that, in the blink of an eye, you turned out to be completely disposable after all and your partner disappears into the sunset with another victim (who, unbeknownst to them, will soon be discarded themselves).

After the "discard," your partner might emerge from the deep silence like the soldier returning from battle, summoning you into his open arms. Sometimes, but not always, narcissists end up trying to get their partners back. They have found that they did, after all, find value in you, even if it was simply in the way you made them feel good about yourselves, and rolled over, like a good dog, to meet their demands and obey their instructions. They do this by pretending to miss them, even though they really just want them back because they need the easy source of supply, and power. During the hoovering phase, they may approach you with the best form of apology they can muster (Arabi, 2016): perhaps a sweet suggestion that you may be oversensitive, or offer a seemingly remorseful confession that maybe they get a little aggressive sometimes, or whatever else they think they did to offend you. If you see this happening after you have left the relationship, or during the devaluation phase, run in the opposite direction, as there is a risk that you will be lured back into the relationship like a moth to the flame. The danger here is that it culminates in the worst-case scenario in which you end up believing that you are in the wrong, apologizing and allowing yourself to be lured back into the sticky web of manipulations (Arabi, 2016). Don't be fooled or drop your guard—it's another act designed especially for you, so that you end up being coaxed back into the relationship to pretend as if nothing had happened to make you want to leave in the first place. The first time you are discarded is the best time to leave for good, although even once you have parted ways, they may still find ways to harass you and ensure they are stringing you along in false hope, because the notion of you getting on with your life independently of them is inconceivable (Arabi, 2016).

So far we have been deconstructing the concept of narcissism, narcissistic abuse and Narcissistic Personality Disorder, so that you can understand your wife, as a narcissist, better. We will continue to unravel the threads of narcissism in the next chapter by further exploring the various types and subtypes that it is divided into.

Chapter 3:

Decoding the Types of

Narcissists

If you thought you had a good grasp of what narcissism is, you couldn't be more wrong. So far, we have made sweeping statements about the nature of narcissists in general, but there is more to narcissism than meets the eye, according to the growing body of knowledge on the topic. With increasing momentum, more and more theorists are becoming immersed in the study of narcissistic pathology. Like any collection of theories that emerge from the corridors of universities and the uncluttered minds of researchers, it is ever growing, ever changing, and becoming more and more refined as we come to recognize the nuances of different narcissists.

We started off with a broad definition of what narcissism is, gave you some clues as to what kinds of traits you could expect in a person who is narcissistic, and proceeded to go into further depth about Narcissistic Personality Disorder as a disorder that is diagnosable in a clinical context. Remember that many of the traits described in the context on the discussion on NPD above are relevant to narcissism in general, but more accurately reflect the challenges that the 'grandiose' narcissist (otherwise known as the 'classic' narcissist) poses to us. In this chapter, we will sojourn into the theory that has developed over the years about other quirks that define grandiose narcissistic people, but we must pay equal attention to other forms of narcissism that may be a little more difficult to recognize as we go about our daily lives.

The concept of narcissism can be deconstructed into different types and subtypes, and we will aim to explore just that in this chapter so that you can differentiate between the different narcissists in order to identify what kind of narcissist your wife might be. The kind of theoretical background provided in this chapter is done in the name of tackling the difficulties you are living in your relationship with your wife, with the most comprehensive knowledge base that is available.

So, let us proceed to unpack the various types and subtypes of narcissism, and to examine them with the keen eye of a scientist unraveling the mysteries of the universe, only the 'universe' in question here is the narcissist and her ego. What can you expect in this chapter? Firstly, there will be a description of three main types of narcissism: grandiose narcissism, vulnerable narcissism, and malignant narcissism. Next, cerebral and somatic narcissism will be explored as subtypes, followed by a brief overview of where covert and overt narcissism fit into the picture. You will also be given an indication of what narcissistic abuse might look like in each of the main types.

Three Types of Narcissism

<u>The Classic Narcissist</u>

If you think that your wife is a grandiose narcissist and that her behavior could potentially be abusive, these are the kinds of signs that you should look out for. Remember that physical abuse is much easier to identify or label than emotional, verbal, or psychological abuse, but the latter can have devastating long-term effects, so the signs are definitely worth looking out for. Chapter five will give you a clearer idea of the signs to look out for in grandiose and vulnerable abuse respectively. I will re-emphasize the importance here of finding social support that can serve to hear you and provide reflection from a group of people who can relate to what you are going through.

The classic narcissist is your textbook narcissist we would all associate with the word 'narcissist.' If you caught her walking in the street or shopping mall, you'd think she was just like anybody else going about her daily business, but an encounter with her would make you think twice about that judgment. Catch her at a party, and she will dazzle you with her overconfident, razor-sharp wit or infallible general knowledge. In conversation, you don't stand a chance of getting a word in edgewise. Flattering, charming, and downright delightful, she can talk you into a daze. Before you know it, you've left the party in awe of this fine specimen of womanhood who embodies nothing but the best of the feminine gender. It wouldn't take you long to become completely enamored, a convert to the cult of 'her.'

Start a relationship with her and it would take somewhat longer for you to realize that the metaphorical music has faded, the lights have dimmed, and you are the last guy at the party waiting for the encore that never comes. You've been duped, conned, used, and abused into thinking her attention came from some deep affection for you. You've been lied to, given the cold shoulder, and ignored, only to be swept up again in a current of adoration and dropped again like a bombshell falling from dizzy heights. You feel drained and alone, like the whole world is against you and you're trapped in a relationship from which you can't escape.

Welcome to the world of the classic narcissist, where the web of lies is proportionally as extensive as her overinflated ego that rises to the sky like a spaceship with neon lights, hovering yet remaining out of reach. With an all-seeing eye, she surveys her dominion and beleaguers her constituents with her opinions, criticisms, insults, and sarcasm. Her presence is so overt that her manipulative ways and ulterior motives become covert, especially to the eyes of the followers that are in her wake. In addition to lacking empathy, Sayers (2018) describes two additional telltale signs that indicate the presence of a narcissist: inflated self-esteem and a reluctance to be open to criticism. Her larger-than-life persona puts all others into orbit, and she would have it no other way. She always takes the credit, her omniscience is astounding (even though, objectively speaking, she is not as smart as she professes), and she uses her strengths to her advantage, no matter the cost to others in her orbit. We've touched briefly on the self-esteem issue, the ego that takes on superhuman proportions. The thing about a narcissist is that their achievements are usually not as great as they profess them to be. While the narcissist is eager to deliver criticism to others, they can't help but respond aggressively when the tables are turned against them, and they may go to great lengths to either verbally attack the person criticizing them or turn the conversation toward their strengths instead. She is a keeper, she will make you believe, and you have to work hard to earn her presence in your life.

Grandiose Narcissistic Abuse

It's important to be aware of the signs of narcissistic abuse. Whether you are being abused by a grandiose, vulnerable, or malignant narcissist, it takes the form of verbal, psychological, or emotional abuse. There have been many cases where the abuse has taken on physical and sexual dimensions as well, but emotional abuse can be harder to spot as it manifests in the words that are said and the facial expressions and body language that is used. The difficulty of recognizing when this kind of abuse is happening is heightened by the nature of your relationship with the narcissist: being under the emotional stress of living with a narcissist and pervasively bombarded by her energetic attack is enough to make you blind to the reality of what is going on. Beyond that, there is also the matter of triangulation that will almost be impossible to penetrate: even if you do recognize that you are being abused, it may be difficult to get anyone to believe you. This kind of abuse can have devastating long-term effects, so look out for the signs.

Abuse can occur with all forms of narcissism, but here are some telltale indications, provided and elaborated upon by Grande (2019a) in his YouTube video, *10 Signs of Grandiose Narcissistic Abuse*. These signs might appear if you are living with a grandiose narcissist particularly. First off, you may be overwhelmed with feelings of being trapped. If you are feeling like there is no way forward or no way out of your marriage, like there is no room for either you or your relationship to grow, this is a sign that you are in a relationship with a grandiose narcissist. In order for a relationship to grow, it would require attention and effort from both parties, for the sake of the relationship as something that is bigger than each individual. But we know that the narcissist's primary point of focus is herself, so that it takes an extreme stretch of the imagination to put you or the relationship before her own ego and selfish motivations. The fact that she steamrolls your opinion, no matter how constructive it may seem in the context of your own needs or the needs of the relationship, not to mention the fact that she won't receive criticism from others, are two examples of reasons why your relationship may feel like it is going nowhere. The truth is that, if you are in a relationship with a narcissist, it probably isn't. As much as you try to give your relationship or yourself a voice, you are attempting to reconcile the irreconcilable. You are attempting to function in and repair a relationship that is purposefully designed against you, and the joke is on you. From the get-go, you have had different goals from the person you married, and they are still different. And in the case of the grandiose narcissist, that probably won't change no matter how hard you try.

So the relationship might not seem to be growing, and a lack of forgiveness plays no small role in this (Grande, 2019a). In a relationship with a narcissist, you will find that the narcissist will keep bringing up mistakes you made in the past. Regardless of what the outcome of that particular misdemeanor was (maybe you resolved the issue, or apologized for it), it will be used against you in an argument until the end of time (Grande, 2019a). Your failings in the past will be used against you as ammunition during arguments. For example, she might bring up the fact that you locked the keys in the car some months ago and use this to remind you how irresponsible or scatterbrained you are.

Another symptom of a relationship that is governed by a narcissistic spouse is if there is limited intellectual stimulation in conversation (Grande, 2019a). Gone are the days of the person you first met—the colorful act she put on display to impress people has turned into a dull gray as you and she both struggle to be heard. The words leave your mouths, but they fly past both of you like shrapnel to be lost in the cacophony of frustration and resentment. You may find that you both manage to express yourself in conversation, but you or your spouse is not hearing what is being said. You are talking across each other. When you leave a verbal exchange, there is no sense that a meaningful conversation has happened, and this can sometimes lead to frustration and make you feel worse—unfulfilled and empty. Tomorrow it will be the same, and no matter how hard you try, you know that your words will fall on deaf ears.

Finally, on top of the trapped feeling that you have that the relationship is not going anywhere, there are certain emotional signs that may appear in you as the victim, like depression or a feeling of hopelessness and being out of control in your life, that can indicate that there is something wrong, even if you can't put words to it (Grande, 2019a). It can even manifest as hatred for your partner, or hatred toward yourself for not leaving the relationship (Grande, 2019a). Of course, it may be that these feelings are part of a mental disorder, or the result of another problem you are experiencing in your life, but if they are occurring in the context of the other information that is provided here, these feelings may just be the proverbial nail in the coffin.

These kinds of feelings can culminate in you thinking malicious thoughts about your partner and hoping that something bad will happen to her (Grande, 2019a). She goes for a ride in the car and you hope she will crash, or she is using the saw and you wish for her to injure herself. This doesn't make you a bad person; it simply describes what you are thinking and feeling about your partner. This reflexive response can say a lot about the state you are in and also provides feedback about the relationship. Wishing harm upon someone indicates that something is wrong and needs addressing.

It may seem bizarre, but it is sometimes the case in these kinds of relationships that the partner who is not a narcissist starts to adopt the same behaviors as the narcissist (Grande, 2019a). For example, you might find that you also struggle with forgiveness and, like your spouse, keep bringing up the past. If the narcissistic person is acting immature, you might start responding to them in kind, not by imitating them intentionally, but rather by subconsciously taking on their behavior patterns so that the entire relationship can start to look immature (Grande, 2019a). So if your partner responds to your criticism by yelling at you, you might gradually start doing the same when you argue.

Bear in mind, as you read these descriptions, that the information provided here is not comprehensive. It should also be pointed out that other factors, not only the occurrence of NPD, could contribute to some of the features mentioned above, and that the features of grandiose narcissistic abuse that are mentioned here could also be present with other kinds of narcissists.

Before we move on to the topic of vulnerable narcissism, I want to visit the topic of the sexual aspect of your relationship with a classic narcissist, and I will do the same when discussing the vulnerable narcissist, as these are the two main types of narcissism that dominate the literature and have a fairly concrete presence in society, compared to the hypothetical nature of malignant narcissism.

In a relationship with the grandiose or vulnerable narcissist, sexual narcissism can become a means of expression for the narcissist where the superficiality of the narcissist extends into the sexual domain (Grande, 2019a). This may not take the form of overt sexual abuse. It can take the form, for example, of the victim of narcissistic abuse being overly submissive with regard to the frequency of intercourse and level of sadism (Grande, 2019a). You may find that you don't derive any satisfaction from the sexual act, and this is because, as it is the case in all other aspects of your life with your partner, you are being used to her own satisfaction, where the word 'satisfaction' here is used less to describe sexual satisfaction than the satisfaction that is obtained from pursuing and dominating you (Grande, 2019a).

There you have it. The grandiose narcissist is an energy vampire who can leave you running on empty, but she is also an energetic force that can be felt across the room. It's a force to be reckoned with. Being in her presence is an energetic assault. It's a tirade that leaves you wanting and leaves no room for your own identity, which you must surrender to the narcissistic beast who revels in taking power from you in the most overt kind of way.

Vulnerable Narcissism

Many of the characteristics that were described in the previous chapter so far yell "grandiose narcissist" in no uncertain terms. But there is another common kind of narcissist that lurks in the shadows unnoticed, sporting the same qualities of egocentrism and self-centeredness but in a more subtle way, a way that is more covert and creeps up behind you, where you end up caught in the narcissistic game, tangled in its confusing web before you know it. This is what is known as the "vulnerable narcissist"—far more sly and surreptitiously manipulative than the classic counterpart who openly and shamelessly flaunts her egotistical tactics for all to see.

Unlike the elaborate grandiose showman, who is almost addicted to being in the spotlight, the vulnerable narcissist has a contrasting aversion to being the center of attention. The vulnerable narcissist finds that there is nothing more repulsive than the arrogant self-centeredness of openly hogging people's attention. However, unbeknownst to them, they have a similarly proportioned ego, and although it may not be fed by capturing the crowd and harnessing the potential to be the ringmaster of the show, it is nevertheless hungry for a different kind of attention.

Like grandiose narcissists, vulnerable narcissists believe they are superior to other people, but the way that they express their need for validation of this takes a slightly different flavor. We saw that the grandiose narcissist, being the extrovert that she is, derives her sense of self worth by claiming the spotlight, taking center stage and openly flaunting herself. She gets the attention she wants by assuming that people have as high a regard for her as she does. On the contrary, the vulnerable narcissist seamlessly shapeshifts into victim mode to attract people's attention, and the tone of her covert plea to people takes the form of an appeal to their pity. Instead of demanding that all eyes are on her in social gatherings, the vulnerable narcissist takes a more introverted approach with her "oh woe is me!" attitude during conversation in an otherwise awkward social encounter.

In this way, the covert narcissist is often prone to neurotic disorders like depression and anxiety and can definitely come across as being depressed, even if they aren't clinically diagnosed as such (Grande, 2019b). Much of their own energy is directed toward self-criticism, but this negative energy is often universal in its application to the extent that you may find that you tire of the company of your spouse quite easily. This pessimism is accompanied by feelings of insecurity and an overarching sense of shame (Grande, 2019b). They would rather be recognized as the unsung hero, martyr, or victim than as an egotistical attention-seeker that she might judge the grandiose narcissist to be.

The approach of the vulnerable narcissist is usually passive aggressive in nature, rather than being outwardly overt in expressing herself (Grande, 2019a). Not having the confidence or courage that the classic narcissist has to openly lash you with her words, you'll feel the sharp stab of her vindictiveness after the fact when you find out that she has gone behind your back to sabotage you. Instead of being the main actor on the stage, the vulnerable narcissist is like a conductor in a grand orchestra, or the director behind the stage show, or the puppeteer pulling the strings. She, like the classic narcissist, likes to maintain control, but she does it from behind the scenes, without wanting to take the 'credit.' This can be contrasted to the grandiose narcissist who takes control, in a social setting, more by dominating conversation and expanding their presence so that it fills up every corner of the room.

The vulnerable narcissist is manipulative and cunning beyond measure. She will guilt-trip you into feeling bad for going out without saying it openly. Or, for example, let's say she is in pain because she insisted on lifting something heavy without asking for help. She might then complain that it was too heavy for her to lift, implying that it was your fault that she didn't ask for help. In this way, she avoids being accountable for her own actions because in her eyes, like in those of the classic narcissist, she can do no wrong.

This type of narcissist steers decisions in the direction she wants them to go by pretending it is for the benefit of others. Instead of being honest about what she wants and providing an explanation or justification, as would be normal in an open, honest relationship, she decides what would be good for others and inserts their opinions into the conversation for them because she knows best. This is a classic case of presenting the image of being the martyr while being secretly motivated by her own interests.

A gossip-monger to the T, the vulnerable narcissist uses words like poison against people who are, permanently or temporarily, not of any use to her (and this includes everyone, including you, if we are honest here). She will mine information under the guise of being trustworthy, friendly, and compassionate, and slyly store that information in her mental memory banks to be used at her discretion in the future (Grande, 2019b). No one is safe from the silver tongue of this narcissist.

It was discussed earlier in this book how success in encouraging a narcissist to get help can be dubious at best, never mind the long journey of recovery that would involve them opening up to the possibility of being wrong. It would be an understatement to say they would be resistant, and that it would be a long, tiresome path for you. The good news is that change for the vulnerable narcissist is more likely than their grandiose and malignant counterparts (Grande, 2019b). Unlike the latter two, the vulnerable narcissist can sometimes suspect that something is not quite right with them, and they may even be willing to get the help they need. However, this is not to say that change will come easily—despite their willingness to make an effort, changes can be dramatic, yet equally fleeting (Grande, 2019b). Through their best efforts, you might start to see a suspension of the weight of the relationship as they put their best foot forward, only to feel it crashing back down as they fall back into old patterns (Grande, 2019b).

If your spouse belongs to this group of narcissists, you will find that she can be hyper critical of herself. She oscillates between having very high self-esteem, that is expressed through confidence, and very low self-esteem, especially when other people are criticizing her. If you recall, the classic narcissist tends to react explosively and aggressively when confronted, as she also abhors the mere notion of having done or said something wrong. The possibility of anyone else being injured or offended by their behavior is of course moot. The vulnerable narcissist also can't tolerate being in the wrong, but will adopt a more injured, self-pitying approach in order to shun accountability. This type of narcissist, like the classic, is a master performer and can put on a very convincing act by playing on your own vulnerabilities. In the case of this narcissist, the vulnerability is your guilt, and for the grandiose, it is fear and shame.

Vulnerable Narcissistic Abuse

Guilt is a powerful emotion. If left unexamined, it can be the driving force behind many actions that have been enabled in nature, ones that are not in your interest. Self-reflection is necessary if you want to nip guilty feelings in the bud. Often people can cause guilt in us by insinuating things, imposing upon us an ungrounded sense of responsibility for something. Feeling guilty or responsible for when things go wrong is a powerful tool that the vulnerable narcissist may use to manipulate you. Some people who are living with narcissists say that they constantly feel as though they are not good enough, as if they constantly have to explain themselves. And the explanation never quite fits the bill. Making everyday choices that are based on guilt is like offering your sanity to the narcissist's ego on a platter. Living in this anxious state for the sake of making someone else happy is not conducive to maintaining good mental, physical and emotional health.

This incitement of guilt can be expressed through an ongoing sense of resentment (Grande, 2019b). Another classic characteristic you will come to recognize in the vulnerable narcissist is that they can be resentful and easily bear a grudge if you fail to meet their demands. Being married to this type of narcissist, or being in a romantic relationship with one, can mean that you are constantly reminded of past mistakes that you have made (Grande, 2019b). No matter how many times you apologize, admit your misdemeanor, or resolve any problems that may have arisen from your mistake, you are not easily forgiven. It is largely due to this reason that you may have a constant sense that you are not liked or are not good enough for your partner. If you are married to this kind of narcissist, you may find that you are constantly walking on eggshells, as your partner seems to harbor an underlying anger that seems ready to explode at the next trigger. You may also find that you have come to know exactly what word or gesture will be that trigger (Grande, 2019b).

If you are married to a vulnerable narcissist, you may notice that along with the feelings of insecurity, or perhaps because of it, there is an element of jealousy that pops up, particularly when your attention is directed toward other people (Grande, 2019b). As we saw earlier, jealousy is also a feature of classic narcissism. The difference is that the jealousy of the vulnerable narcissist is motivated by underlying fears of inferiority, which the grandiose narcissist would be jealous of because your attention is on someone other than her. In cases where you do spend time with others, the narcissist may try to elicit guilt from you for being away for so long (Grande, 2019b). This possessiveness and over-attachment is a feature of vulnerable narcissism in particular (Grande, 2019b).

Living with a vulnerable narcissist, you may have noticed your wife has a tendency to accuse you of things that she has no evidence of, and also to start arguments with you in which she is portrayed as the victim, despite possible evidence to the contrary (Grande, 2019b). A relationship that is marred by narcissistic abuse may also be characterized as having few, if any, productive arguments that amount to something or which have a conclusion. Sometimes the narcissistic partner in a relationship will start an argument simply for the sake of it, or for the purpose of causing you pain (Grande, 2019b).

The narcissist we are talking about here has listening skills that can be likened to the classic narcissist—that is to say, very bad ones. The defining difference here is that the vulnerable narcissist pretends to be a good listener, and has mastered the art of appearing to be listening to what you are saying while her mind is elsewhere (Grande, 2019b). This is yet another reason why it can be difficult to label this kind of person as narcissistic—due to these kinds of surreptitious, manipulative streaks that appear to be something they are not.

Another feature that this type of narcissism has in common with grandiose narcissism is the potential for sexual narcissism, as mentioned before, where the sexual act and sexual pursuit becomes simply another way for the narcissist to exert control over you (Grande, 2019a). This takes place not necessarily in a physical way, but in the principle of perhaps using sex as an object with which you can be manipulated and using the submissive you. In this case, the point is not so much physical dominance as it is making you prove your loyalty and love for them (Grande, 2019b).

Malignant Narcissism

One only has to look at the Ted Bundys and John Wayne Gacys of the world to know that these guys operate on the fringes of society, lurk in the gray areas of what is and isn't acceptable and skulk in the shadows of what we consider humane and moral. These are admittedly extreme cases, but are the modern-day archetypes or scapegoats upon which society streamlines its unacceptable, shadowy dark side. Most malignant narcissists are not so extreme, but they are not shy in bending society's norms and laws to suit their needs. In this respect, they go above and beyond the vulnerable and grandiose narcissists who, while expecting the world to bend to their requirements, will probably not push the envelope so far as to break the law.

Malignant narcissism is a mysterious beast. Mysterious, because technically it isn't a diagnosable disorder, and experts themselves are undecided about what exactly it means (Grande, 2019c). Beastly, because a malignant narcissist is widely considered a menace to society of the worst kind, and you will see why in a minute.

The term "malignant narcissist" was first used in the 1960s by Erich Fromm (Grande, 2019c). Since then, many different theories have been proposed regarding its meaning, and still there is no consensus. Kernberg came up with the idea that what he called "Malignant Personality Disorder" is between Antisocial Personality Disorder and Narcissistic Personality Disorder on a spectrum, and that it also features on a different spectrum somewhere between NPD and psychopathy (Grande, 2019c). Other models suggest malignant narcissism is a comorbid presentation of NPD, which means that it can occur simultaneously with NPD (Grande, 2019c).

It is beyond the scope of this book to go into the intricacies of each theory. It is safe to conclude, though, that most models suggest that there is some kind of overlap between NPD and antisocial personality disorder, and some even allude to the inclusion of sadism in the definition of malignant narcissism (Grande, 2019c).

You already have knowledge of what a narcissist and Narcissistic Personality Disorder is. However, to get a clearer picture of what a malignant narcissist might look like, taking into account this idea that it is somehow related to the disorders mentioned above, in terms of their thoughts, feelings and actions, it is necessary to explore the kinds of traits people with Antisocial Personality Disorder exhibit. According to the DSM-5 (2013), this disorder is diagnosed when:

"A. A pervasive pattern of disregard for and violation of the rights of others, occurring since age 15 years, as indicated by three (or more) of the following:

1. Failure to conform to social norms with respect to lawful behaviors, as indicated by repeatedly performing acts that are grounds for arrest.
2. Deceitfulness, as indicated by repeated lying, use of aliases, or conning others for personal profit or pleasure.
3. Impulsivity or failure to plan ahead.
4. Irritability and aggressiveness, as indicated by repeated physical fights or assaults.
5. Reckless disregard for safety of self or others.
6. Consistent irresponsibility, as indicated by repeated failure to sustain consistent work behavior or honor financial obligations.
7. Lack of remorse, as indicated by being indifferent to or rationalizing having hurt, mistreated, or stolen from another.

B. The individual is at least age 18 years.

C. There is evidence of conduct disorder with onset before age 15 years.

D. The occurrence of antisocial behavior is not exclusively during the course of schizophrenia or bipolar disorder."

You can see that disorder is characterized by a number of different symptoms that include things like aggression, lying, criminal activity, general irresponsibility displayed in a lack of concern for self and others, and impulsivity, as well as the absence of feeling guilty about any of this kind of behavior or mistreatment of others (DSM-5, 2013). They have a blatant disregard for the rules of society and social mores and will stop at nothing to achieve their desired goals, provided there is no risk of getting caught.

In order to understand some of the other factors that define a malignant narcissist, it is also important to also describe the meaning of sadism. Some have argued that malignant narcissism also contains an element of "egosyntonic sadism" (Grande, 2019c). Sadism refers to when someone enjoys hurting others. Egosyntonic means that there is an acceptance of the behavior that occurs. When someone is egosyntonically sadistic, it means that they are aware of the harm they have caused and are ok with the fact that they have caused it: their behavior is consistent with their values, therefore, there is no remorse (Grande, 2019c). There is no dissonance between what is considered acceptable, and the behavior that is enacted. People who are sadistic may do something that is heinous and unacceptable to the moral system that governs most other people's behavior, but do not feel the slightest twinge of guilt because it is consistent with their own values. Someone who is slightly narcissistic and not egosyntonically sadistic might do something that is regarded as immoral, but then feel bad about it.

It is obvious that there is no clear-cut, universally accepted definition of what malignant narcissism is, but hopefully you have a better idea of what it might entail when compared to the other forms of narcissism we have already discussed. Remember that this 'strain' of narcissism is only a hypothetical model, and is not included as an official disorder in the DSM-5 (Grande, 2019c). But you can see that this type of narcissism goes above and beyond the relatively innocent antics of the other two types. Malignant narcissism spells trouble with a capital T for the people in the narcissist's life and society at large.

Subtypes of Narcissism

The three narcissists mentioned above (grandiose, vulnerable, and malignant), are three of the primary types of narcissism. In this section , we will lay out the different subtypes. The first distinction that will be made is between the cerebral and somatic narcissist. Before we move on to the next chapter, we will also touch on covert and overt narcissistic subtypes and how they relate to the types of narcissism that are described above.

Cerebral Narcissists

All narcissists are either cerebral or somatic. They usually tend toward being more dominant in either one or the other, and revert to the alternative during crisis, but this way of subdividing the different types of narcissism is all-encompassing (Vankin, 2014). One cannot be neither a cerebral or a somatic narcissist. This way of categorizing the narcissists refers to the object they use to obtain their narcissistic supply. That is, they either use their intelligence or their bodies as the object through which they can obtain validation about their presumed superiority. Dr. Sam Vankin (2014) points out that all narcissists express their narcissistic tendencies through their bodies and/or their intellectual capacities. These have been labeled by experts as the somatic and cerebral subtypes of narcissism. All narcissists have qualities of both of these subtypes and can oscillate between the two, but they usually have one dominant subtype that you will come to recognize, while the qualities of the recessive subtype will only come into play if the dominant type takes a knock or if the narcissist is struggling with a life crisis (Vaknin, 2014).

Let us start with an exposé on the cerebral narcissist. The sneaky thing about cerebral narcissists is that they can make you feel like they are more intelligent than everyone else is, even if they aren't (Ramani, 2020). While highly intelligent and knowledgeable people can be boastful, and indeed narcissistic, the genius of the narcissist is not necessarily his expertise on a subject, but rather making people believe they are an expert.

You may be able to spot a cerebral narcissist by looking out for a large audience that is starstruck by a shower of uncomfortably technical words that hypnotizes them into the illusion that the narcissist is the go-to guy for the topic under discussion. Little does the audience know, the narcissist is deriving much satisfaction from having them under his spell, using their fickleness to feed his or her ego. In this way, the narcissist gets a kick out of being seen as the most intelligent person in the group, even if it isn't necessarily true. Their arrogance tends to smother people's contribution to the conversation, so that what may have had the potential for being a constructive, animated conversation turns into a stage show, or rather a lecture being delivered by the expert (Ramani, 2020). It takes a sinister turn from what could have been an engaging, enthusiastic verbal jousting or debate, into a scene from which the audience departs dazzled and drained.

However, you should not make the mistake of thinking that you need to go to an intellectual conference to witness the glory and supposed omniscience of a cerebral narcissist in action, although these are good places for narcissists who are well-educated to hang out as it is the perfect place for one to show off their education, especially if they studied at a prestigious institution (Ramani, 2020). If they have been well-educated, the narcissist loves for people to know this; remember that they have a considerable regard for being of a high status and associating themselves with people and institutions that have a good reputation.

Still, these narcissists don't need to be highly qualified to flaunt their knowledge, and they can judge people to be intellectually inferior with regard to their knowledge about sport, art, wine...or anything for that matter (Ramani, 2020). The narcissist unfortunately does not have the emotional or social intelligence to allow others to enter into the conversation, nor does she want to allow it to be a two-way conversation (Ramani, 2020). Even if someone did get a word in edgewise, the narcissist would always have something more valuable to say. This is the classic steamroller effect that narcissists can have on other people. Narcissists' partners tend to be invalidated in this way and end up flattened on the pavement, either because it would take too much energy to interject meaningfully (and they would probably emerge from this even more invalidated), or because they feel threatened. If you are in a relationship with a cerebral narcissist, you may feel embarrassed by this kind of behavior, but of course the narcissist is completely oblivious to your feelings.

This type of narcissist can be a grandiose narcissist, or a vulnerable narcissist who has something to prove (Ramani, 2020). In the same way as a narcissist in the workplace might steal someone else's work or say something bad about another employee, the cerebral narcissist makes others look bad by stifling their voice as if doing so can make the narcissist look relatively good. This emphasizes the need of the narcissist to build upon her self-worth through the validation or attention of others. Unfortunately, though, she never reaches the point where she has a solid sense of self worth: there is no genuine sense of self-acceptance, so that all the attention and compliments and high self-esteem in the world are never enough, and the behavior keeps repeating, perpetually filling the void that can never be filled.

By doing this, the narcissist builds a superficial following of people who put on a similarly shallow and misleading front, and the quality of relationships with such people can be proportionally meaningless. An outsider may be able, at this point, to recognize what is happening here, but that may not be true for the people who are being duped, largely because this kind of behavior is perfectly acceptable and justified to them.

We referred earlier in the chapter of the sexual aspect of narcissists, specifically with reference to grandiose and vulnerable narcissists. There is no reason why the eccentricities of narcissists should exclude their sexual lives. According to Vankin (2014), both cerebral and somatic narcissists (i.e. all narcissists) are essentially in love with themselves. The cerebral narcissist is often celibate, even if they are in a relationship, and often prefers to masturbate rather engage in the complexity of a sexual act with another person (Vaknin, 2014). Behold the one-dimensionality of the sexual act that, even through the most physically intimate act, can make you feel completely alienated.

Somatic Narcissist

In contrast to the narcissist who places his priority on his intelligence (which can be either real or imagined), in the case of the somatic narcissist, it is the body that is ultimately used to gain narcissistic supply instead of the mind. Many people mistakenly think that this refers to sexual activity and associate the somatic narcissist with a sex addict, but this is not the case (Vaknin, 2014).

Although it may be possible for a narcissist to also be a sex addict (or any other kind of addict for that matter), the latter is not a condition for diagnosis of Narcissistic Personality Disorder. When it comes to the topic of sex, the thrill, with the somatic narcissist, is not so much in the act or frequency of sex, but rather in the pursuit of it (Vaknin, 2014). Winning you over and you becoming the object of her sexual attention is the thing that brings her a sense of being powerful and in control. From this, she derives a sense of being special, worthy of attention, and generally irresistible.

It should come as no surprise that the somatic narcissist does not engage in sex for the purpose of enjoying intimacy, affection, or emotional connection. Rather, she sees you as an object for her personal use, the means by which she can attain sexual pleasure (Vaknin, 2014). Like the cerebral narcissist, the somatic narcissist is essentially in love with herself (Vaknin, 2014). You are the prize she has won, and she can use you as her plaything to subjugate to achieve a particular end (i.e. sexual satisfaction). Among the other factors mentioned here, the subjugation plays a big role in giving her the narcissistic supply that she needs. When the somatic narcissist has sadistic or psychopathic tendencies (as a malignant narcissist might have), physical harm of the other person can enter into the equation as well, where the objectification of the other person's body can be taken to the extreme of mutilation (Vaknin, 2014). If you have not yet noticed these underlying motivations and attitudes during your sexual encounters with your wife, you may still feel as though sex is impersonal, unfulfilling and draining, which can be a telltale sign that sexual narcissism is at play here.

You have now become familiar with the mental aspect behind the more intimate sexual aspect of your experience with your wife. How else can you recognize a somatic narcissist? Well, somatic narcissists are extremely body-conscious. For starters, she is not hard to recognize in a conversation. She may openly advertise her sexual exploits and conquests or dominate conversations about her diet or achievements at the gym (Vaknin, 2014).

This may be expressed in the form of continually taking photos of herself or looking in the mirror. She might be obsessed with her body, continually dieting, talking about her diet and her physical assets, buying clothes that conform to the latest fashion, or spending hours on personal hygiene and make-up. A somatic narcissist might be fanatical about their health—they might spend hours a day body-building or exercising (Vaknin, 2014). On the other hand, the body might be the object of attention through hypochondria—always thinking about or worrying that something is physically wrong with them (Vaknin, 2014).

Covert Narcissist

Along with the cerebral versus somatic distinction, there is another set of subtypes that narcissism can be separated into: overt and covert narcissism. The former is, more often than not, associated with grandiose narcissism, and the latter usually goes hand-in-hand with vulnerable narcissism. We will briefly describe both before moving on to the next chapter. Remember that all narcissists have a few core characteristics in common. For example, all narcissists lack empathy, have what seems to be an exaggerated opinion of themselves as superior to others, and have a pathological need for attention and need to assert control. What distinguishes one type or subtype from another is the object used as the focus of attention to get the validation they need (somatic versus cerebral), and the specific methods of manipulation used to gain control (grandiose, vulnerable, and malignant, and covert versus overt narcissism).

The covert narcissist is as the name implies: subtle and surreptitious. Cox (2019) describes the typical covert narcissist as having six defining features. Firstly, they are smug. Despite remaining silent and introverted, their significant presence can be felt by their judgemental attitude and air of superiority that they naturally emit. They may communicate their harsh opinion of whatever you have to say with you, but they will probably drop hints rather than express their views outright. If you think that these narcissists think they are better than you, you'd be right. This becomes evident in conversation, for example, by the way they disengage from what you are saying. While they don't outright tell you their sheer boredom when you speak, they don't hold back in the way they express it through body language. The airs and graces of this narcissist are hard to miss, despite the fact that they adopt more of the observer role. Although both the grandiose and vulnerable narcissist believe they are inherently superior to you, and anyone else for that matter, the vulnerable narcissist will not be as explicit in reminding people about this. Instead of openly boasting, she may refuse to do work that she considers unworthy of her attention, or she might think that being in the presence of certain inferior individuals is demeaning to her awesome presence This sense of superiority and god-given right to define the rules, and the associated sense of entitlement that defines her actions, may also manifest as a reluctance or outright refusal to socialize with others, or even look after the kids if she has something better to do with her precious time. In the home environment, the covert narcissist might also think that she is above performing certain duties or household chores.

The second trait of the covert narcissist, as described by Cox (2019), that is worth mentioning here is the proclivity for sensitivity. We mentioned this hyper-sensitivity in the context of the discussion on vulnerable narcissists, and the same information that was divulged with regard to vulnerable narcissism applies to this subtype. We will simply add here that when criticized, they tend to take things personally. Instead of taking on criticism as constructive, they feel threatened by the idea of someone pointing out what is wrong with them.

Thirdly, and if you recall this same quality applies for vulnerable narcissists, is a preference for passive-aggressive expressions of hostility as a way of maintaining control (Cox, 2019). There are many ways that passive-aggressive behavior can manifest, one of them being through the way that they talk to you. They will habitually bring you down for no apparent reason and interpret things that you do or say through a veil that is tinged with toxicity. These muddy waters that you wade through can start to cake you with the mud of the foul comments made by your partner that are meant to weigh you down and punish you for all the times you have injured their ego (which sometimes doesn't take too much). When you emerge from the swampy soup of criticism, you feel heavy, and breaking free from the narcissist's aura of negativity can be challenging indeed.

Another effective way that passive-aggressive behavior is employed is also through the use of words as weapons, this time in the form of poorly disguised humor that can take on the tone of sarcasm (Cox, 2019). When these kinds of comments are made, especially in front of others, you can end up feeling bullied and downright stupid as you are unfairly and publicly lambasted under the pretense of humor, all in the name of making you pay for not meeting the narcissist's impossible standards.

Next, blame is an extremely convenient way for the covert narcissist to shift attention from their own wrongdoing to others (Cox, 2019). It's a very handy way of making others think that someone else should be held responsible for their own behavior and distracting them from the real matter at hand.

Sabotage is a more obvious way for the narcissist to ensure control over you and protect her ego. This type of narcissist will go the extra mile to intentionally set you up for failure by doing things like using information against you, for example.

As you can see, when compared to the grandiose narcissist, this type of narcissist is shy, and generally not up for social situations in the same way as the classic narcissist is. Vulnerable narcissists, in general, try to avoid social settings. There could be a number of reasons for this, including anxiety (we have already seen how this type of narcissist is prone to anxiety and depression), fear of being judged and coming off second-best.

Overt Narcissism

Guarino (n.d.) describes the overt narcissist as unashamed of the fact that she manipulates and controls people for her own personal gain. She makes no attempt to hide that fact, or the methods she uses to control others around her. She might have some awareness of the fact that she uses people, but expresses no remorse over this reality and exploits others in her personal pursuits without recognizing the effect her actions have on other people. The overt narcissist, like the classic narcissist, likes to be the center of attention, and will reap the attention of others by showing off and putting others down in an extroverted fashion, even if it means fabricating truths to make her look good. Having no remorse for the fact that she craves power, control, and attention, the overt narcissist will blatantly impose her power upon others to intimidate them and prove her worth. Overt narcissism is often equated with grandiose narcissism, so refer to that section to clarify the meaning of overt narcissism.

In conclusion, this chapter has given you a summary of the different types of narcissism, how they would appear in everyday life, and also how they would appear in an abusive marriage (we will further explore what narcissistic abuse means in chapter five). As you have seen in this chapter, a distinction needs to be made based on the unique qualities between different types and subtypes of narcissists. Before you can know how to draw a line in the sand to safeguard your own personal space, you need to establish what type of narcissist your wife is. Only then can you know how to most effectively approach your conundrum of how to retain your sanity living in the claustrophobic environment of the narcissist. In the next chapter, we will look more closely into the reasons why narcissists behave in these ways from the point of view of their physical make-up and personal histories. We will also dive deep into the nitty-gritty thought processes of what might be occurring in the cogs of the narcissist's mental and emotional machine as a byproduct of these causal factors. Now that you have reached the end of the chapter, can you tell which type of narcissist your wife is? If not, read chapters one through three again and take some time to actively reflect on this question. As for the next chapter, we will delve into the discourse of the development of this mental disorder and how it can come to be.

Chapter 4:

Beyond Smoke and Mirrors

The narcissist is like a magician in the sense that she is like a showman using smoke and mirrors to create the illusion of how she wants others to see her. In this chapter, we will start to systematically remove all of the magician's tools of the trade so that we can see the real person behind the facade. We will do this by exploring the ways in which childhood experiences and human biology might explain her narcissistic traits and, in the following chapter, we will analyze what could possibly be going on in the deep backwaters of the narcissist's mind and heart (in the context of what we cover in this chapter).

Like the other theories we have mentioned in this book so far, ideas about the etiology of narcissism are similarly tentative. In other words, nobody really knows with absolute certainty what causes narcissism, or any other mental disorder for that matter. Ongoing study by various researchers, though, has resulted in a number of theoretical frameworks being posited and fleshed out, that can help us glean a semblance of clarity about how people who are seemingly devoid of empathy come to be this way, or rather what conditions are usually necessary for a person to grow up to have extreme narcissistic traits that are beyond the norm.

While specific causes have not yet been scientifically proven, numerous studies have been done that point in the direction of certain risk factors that could be involved in the development of NPD. There is a general movement toward suggesting, with some degree of evidence, that the factors at work are a complicated interplay of three components: environmental factors (especially relating to experiences during childhood), brain structure, and genetics.

Before we get into the nitty-gritty details of each of these factors and explore the relationship they might have with one another, I'd like to emphasize the point that the purpose of including this information here is not to invoke a guilt-ridden sense of sympathy toward the narcissist in your life. At the start of this book, we asked whether narcissists deserve our sympathy in the face of a growing narrative that paints victims as the people toward which any sense of sympathy or compassion should be directed. In the same way that we approach people who have other mental disorders, we must surely tap into our own capacity for empathy, recognize that narcissists are human too, and assume that, like others who are diagnosed with mental disorders (as they are labeled in the DSM-5), these problems are, to a large extent, determined by dysfunctional family relationships and traumatic childhood experiences and, to put it more generally, factors that are essentially beyond the control of the narcissist. And it turns out that they are, as you will soon find out.

This doesn't imply that we should sympathize with the narcissist at our own expense, but it is a fair assessment to make. Narcissists can't help being the way they are. Understanding why narcissists are the way they are can help us to handle the situation we are in, in a more objective way that allows us to see that the way they treat us is not personal, even though at times it can feel as though it is.

Environmental Factors

Psychology literature, and indeed websites on the internet, are awash with a cornucopia of different opinions, theories, and sometimes conflicting information about the human psyche. Without getting into too much detail about the history of some of the debates that have been raging in the world of psychology and psychiatry, and that are always changing according to what is happening in the cultural, political, and economic climate of the time, there is one debate that is of particular relevance here. It relates to the relationship between the natural physical state of the individual (referred to in the said debate as 'nature'), and the environment in which that individual finds him or herself as an infant, child, and adolescent (this is referred to as 'nurture'). One of the most enduring topics that has been the subject of debate for decades regards the nature of the relationship between environmental factors and biological factors in contributing to the development of pathologies of the mind, or mental disorders. This is fondly referred to as the "nature/nurture debate." It raises the question of the extent to which physical factors are responsible for problems with mental health, compared to the role that cultural and social factors play in the etiology of mental problems.

It is a widely agreed-upon fact that past experiences play a fundamental role in the etiology of dysfunction that manifests later on in adolescence or adulthood, and this idea has always been given the spotlight in theories in developmental psychology. Back when it first became an issue, much significance was attributed to the role of the family in being the main factor contributing to the development of mental illness. Other contextual factors, like social support and religious background, were not considered to be hugely significant. Indeed, in the early days of this debate regarding the origins of mental illness, most of the blame was put on the mother in particular. The mother was regarded as largely, if not entirely, responsible for the mental acuity of the child (Vaknin, 2020).

Even in more recent theories, the importance of the role that the family plays is considered an inarguable truth, with no shadow of doubt. It is of course the case that the quality of parenting can play a pivotal role in the mental health and well-being of children and their potential to develop into healthy adults who are capable of establishing meaningful relationships with others. The family is still regarded as one of the most important key players in determining the mental health of a child. However, today the onus lies on the parents within the wider cultural, social, religious, economic, and wider familial context.

On the one hand, it is thought that parents can literally teach their children to become narcissists. This may not happen in an explicit way, but the parents may be narcissists themselves. In the vocabulary used by people in the field, people's brains are 'plastic.' They can be, and are, easily conditioned. Children are especially vulnerable to influence from the outside world— indeed, they rely upon it to receive information that should assist them in surviving and thriving in the world. The plastic brains of children can be molded and shaped; the people they become are inevitably determined by the information they receive through their senses. They model the behavior of the people they are closest to. The narcissist is no exception. If a child grows up with narcissistic parents who treat people like objects to be used at their discretion, then she will learn that it is ok to treat people in such a fashion.

This is one theory that has been proposed to explain the role of 'nurture' in the development of mental disorders, the role of childhood experiences. On the other hand, it is widely accepted that children are naturally narcissistic, but that, given the correct environment and parenting styles, they should grow out of being this way and start to develop skills that enable them to include other people in their landscape of possibility, to recognize their own needs in addition to their own, and to relate to them on an emotional level. According to this perspective, a healthy child is a narcissistic one who is provided with the correct environment for him or her to outgrow these traits, put their own egos aside, and recognize their place in a larger community. Difficult experiences when they are children, even traumatic ones, prevent them from moving beyond this stage, and so children with abnormalities in their upbringing never develop emotional maturity that allows them to surpass the narcissistic stage (Arabi, 2016). These children then take these narcissistic tendencies with them into adulthood.

Traumatic experiences that might affect a child's inability to move beyond the narcissistic phase vary in nature. For example, children rely solely on their parents to provide for their most basic needs. If this trust is broken, a child can grow up to be in a world of pain, struggling to develop meaningful relationships with people, and developing defense mechanisms that may protect them from pain that is induced by other people, but which can have long-term detrimental effects. In this situation, the idea is that a narcissist could develop from an upbringing in which the child experienced a betrayal of the trust of the primary caregivers, for example. According to this theory, the narcissist's hard and offensive exterior is like a crusty scar that has developed on a deep wound, or a set of armor that has been adorned to protect them from further harm. But we know that beneath the armor is a person with flesh and blood who is just as susceptible to being wounded as we are, if not more so, despite the appearance.

The way in which the concept of growing up with narcissists intertwines with this second idea that was proposed in the above paragraph (the experience of trauma as a child) can be complex. The two might go hand in hand, but they might not, and this also depends on whether other protective factors are present. Distrust in primary caregivers could potentially take place in a variety of ways. Parents could, for example, be physically abusive. Neglect (Arabi, 2016) can also be a form of trauma resulting in a distrust of others, as the parents are the first and most intimate people a child relates to in his or life and therefore the relationship with them sets the template for future relationships.

Not only would a child imitate the behaviors of narcissists, but having narcissistic parents can be a devastating experience as well, causing trauma that has an adverse effect on a child's ability to become a mature adult. From what you have learned about narcissists, imagine growing up under the thumb of one or two narcissists. We know that narcissists have a certain fondness for people and things that might be said to have a high status, that they can be quite competitive, and that they use people. This might put pressure on the child to perform well enough at an activity that their parent likes at the expense of experiencing a happy childhood. It could translate into a state of anxiety for the child in which they constantly feel like they are competing with their parent, and it could make them feel like they are a trophy to be exhibited rather than a person deserving of love and affection.

Even without narcissistic parents, divorce can also result in the child being treated as an object or used to obtain leverage in the parents' battle of the wills (Arabi, 2016). In the circumstances of parental divorce or separation, the child might feel a sense of rejection, as if they have to win the love of one or both parents.

Another factor that comes into play, especially in the case of divorce, is whether there are other children in the picture and the dynamic that the siblings have with one another. There could be half-siblings, step-siblings, or adopted siblings, and this might add to a sense of competition and sibling rivalry that is geared toward winning the affection and approval of the parents.

Parenting strategies can also play a significant role in determining the presence and permanence of narcissistic qualities in a child, and their propensity to be carried forward into adulthood (Arabi, 2016). In the literature, there are a number of different parenting styles. Two of these can be said to be at the extreme ends of a scale representing the level of discipline. One of these, the overindulgent parent, provides the child with too much leeway to do whatever they want. The parents see this child as the apple of their eye, the golden child. As discussed earlier, the child is influenced by the beliefs and attitudes of the parents, so in this case they take on this belief that it is ok to expect others to treat them like they are special or different to others and that they can push other people's boundaries, take advantage of people, and bend the rules to suit their wants and needs. They start to have a sense of entitlement. They are given permission to do as they wish without ever learning to take into consideration the impact this might have on others or the fact that there might be consequences to their actions. The narcissist starts to seed itself in the child, and by the time they are adults, they are accustomed to calling the shots and getting whatever they want, come hell or high water, because they were never given the opportunity to learn to develop emotional awareness as children.

Arabi (2016) describes a link between neglectful backgrounds and vulnerable narcissists, and overindulgent parents and grandiose narcissists who have an unrealistic sense of entitlement. It isn't necessarily the case that there is a causal relationship between these two styles of parenting and these types of narcissism, but Arabi (2016) claims that there are risk factors associated with these styles of parenting.

Children who are neglected on a physical or emotional level can carry this trauma into their adolescence and adult lives, and carry with them the effect of a childhood that is starved of love and affection. It is through the manipulative, cunning, and pitiful ways of the vulnerable narcissist that they find the attention that they never received in childhood. They learned early on that they had to develop ways to get what they wanted and needed, and found that they could do so by working in the shadows to choreograph events and people to get what they want and need.

However, children who are treated like they are special, who are overindulged, tend to end up with a sense of entitlement that reduces their capacity for empathizing with others (Arabai, 2016). Their exaggerated sense of self-importance and self-entitlement comes directly from this view that their parents have of them (Arabi, 2016). The parents think they are special, and they assimilate this view of themselves and start to believe it too. Their parents do not teach them to establish boundaries as children; they are taught that it is ok for them to break rules and norms that apply to everyone else.

In addition to the above, Grande (2018) suggests the following as elements in the family (or more specifically, parenting) that could also have an effect on the development of narcissism:

- Having a childhood in which the parents give excessive praise, coupled with equally extreme judgment or criticism
- Lack of empathy in parents
- Parents who exhibited approval and love only in response to having certain abilities or appearance
- Inconsistent parenting
- Parents who place a lot of value on success, achievement and having a high status
- Emotional abuse
- Failure of parents to identify and regulate emotions.

The focus so far in this discussion has been on the role that the parents play, because it is a significant one. There is a danger here of attributing full responsibility for the development of narcissism in children to the parents. Other factors that could contribute toward the development of narcissism include the larger family structure the child grows up in, friendships, childhood experiences outside the family context, the media, and the cultural and religious environment. These could count as protective factors: if a child has narcissistic or neglectful parents, for example, being part of a loving, empathetic circle of family and friends can compensate for the lack of love that a child experiences from the parents.

On the other hand, these factors could instead make the development of narcissism more likely. If the child grows up in a culture in which competition is favored amongst peers, for example, and there is no caring support from the extended family, narcissistic traits could consolidate in the child. This is where the broader perspective that is provided by evolutionary biology can come into play. Instead of focusing on an explanation for narcissism that takes the microcosmic approach of designating responsibility to the family, this theory says that narcissism is developing to ensure survival of the species. The argument here is that, in a society in which narcissism gives the individual better chance of survival (which in some cultures, it does), then narcissism can be seen as a positive trait, one that is ultimately favorable for the perpetuation of the species. It is the perfect example of "survival of the fittest." If narcissism makes you more likely to give you the edge in a job interview and win the girl over, then narcissism will prevail.

Let us return to the nature/nurture debate and the question of how much the environment causes narcissism compared to biological factors. We've taken a look at the role that primary caregivers and their parenting styles can affect children growing up, within the broader cultural climate. Now we will turn our gaze to the physical elements that might be involved, starting by investigating the way that the physical structure of the brain might reflect, or affect, the presence of narcissistic traits in an individual.

Contrary to the theories described in the previous section regarding the significance of the environment, some studies have shown that narcissism can also emerge in people who grew up in loving, functional homes. This, then, begs the question: how is that possible, if the theories suggesting that families play a large role in the development of narcissism, or at least in the way that narcissistic traits seem to linger on in certain individuals in adulthood, are to be believed? It is in cases like these that the unavoidable reality appears: other factors are involved.

And so, in the wake of decades of analyzing and promoting the idea that upbringing is of fundamental importance, theorists have been forced to turn their attention to the idea of the occurrence of mental illness as something that is beyond the control of mere mortals, that endures beyond time and the itchy fingers of the man-made or cultural environment. The desire for man to be held accountable for madness through the enviro-centric approach described above is squashed by the possibility of an explanation that belongs in the realms of biology. Madness is something that can be accounted for by returning to that most fragile of entities which is made of organic matter: the human body.

Brain Structure and Genetics

Vaknin (2020) gives a comprehensive account of the context in which the question of the physical body in determining mental illness has arisen. There has recently developed an interest in researching the way the physical body might affect mental health, where brain structure and genetics are considered to be worth investigating as the potential cause of mental disorders. Much of the interest in this area has concerned mood disorders, but momentum is growing for studies pertaining to the body and its relationship with narcissism as well. Vaknin (2020) states that numerous studies have been done that reveal differences in the brain structure and genetics of those who have personality disorders such as Borderline Personality Disorder and Antisocial Personality Disorder compared to people who don't have these disorders. Theorists have inferred from these research results that the same differences would apply to people with narcissistic tendencies. Other reasons as to why the trend has started gravitating toward a more biological perspective are the fact that previous theories emphasizing the importance of the mother in causing schizophrenia have been proved inaccurate, and the fact that there is a tendency for people in the field to transform psychology into an enterprise that fits into the world of medicine (Vaknin, 2020). With that, there is an emerging reductionist approach that wants a single solution to whatever question is at hand (Vaknin, 2020).

Regardless of the reason for this change, there is evidence of a relationship between biological factors and narcissism that has been revealed in the physical differences in the brain structure of narcissists when compared to people who have empathy and compassion (Grande, 2018). Numerous studies have been done to compare the physical structure of the brain of people with Narcissistic Personality Disorder with those who do not have NPD (Grande, 2018). Findings have not been consistent among people who have the disorder, but the areas of the brain that have shown differences are the areas of the brain that are responsible for the regulation of emotions as well as the region of the brain that is associated with social behavior (Grande, 2018). If you compare what these brain scans reveal with what we know about narcissists, the results are consistent (Grande, 2018).

Grande (2018) points out that we should bear in mind that these results do not necessarily prove that there is a *causal* relationship here; they simply show that there is a *correlation* between NPD and certain areas of the brain. We should also not rule out the possibility that NPD causes a change in brain structure, rather than the reverse happening (Grande, 2018).

So, while there is an almost obvious need to include personal history, environment, and upbringing in the etiological explanation of mental illness, it is hard to argue with the tangible results from studies that have conformed to protocol that is accepted in the scientific community that make such results valid and reliable.

We have spoken about the relationship between brain structure and narcissism (and other personality disorders), but what about genetics? There is a growing movement toward doing research that investigates the role of the genes in contributing to the development of mental disorders, and the results tend to point in the direction of there being a correlation between the two. For example, in one study on the heritability of personality disorders in twins, it was shown that heritability of narcissistic traits was up to 64% ("Genetic and Environmental Contributions..", 1993).

As a result of the extensive ongoing study of this topic, there is a general consensus that males are more likely to develop narcissistic traits than females (although this is not to say that narcissism never develops in females during the transition into adulthood). It has also been widely agreed upon that narcissism can be related to depression and anxiety, especially during stressful events, or times of crisis.

Paul Meehl has come up with one theory that integrates the almost obvious need to include the biological approach with the equally incontrovertible truth that, when it comes to mental health, childhood experiences matter. During his study of Schizophrenia, Meehl came up with what he called the "diathesis-stress model" (Vaknin, 2020). This theory proposes that, instead of people being born with a certain mental illness, they have a genetic predisposition for one mental disorder or another, or at least traits associated with mental disorders (Vaknin, 2020). This aspect in Meehl's theory refers to "diathesis" (Vaknin, 2020). According to this theory, when an individual experiences certain stressors, these latent or potential disorders or traits become activated or triggered to emerge in full form and find expression (Vaknin, 2020). These stressors could be anything from parents getting divorced to being bullied at school, physical illness, and everything in between (Vaknin, 2020).

The theory goes on to say that even if both of these conditions are met, that is, if a person has genetic predisposition toward a mental illness and has the misfortune of being under extreme stress at some point in their lives, they could still escape the clutches of the manifestation of a mental illness if they have a solid set of protective factors in their lives (Vaknin, 2020). So while many of us, even the likes of you and I, may have these vulnerable genes lurking in the dark unseen recesses of our physical constitution, the good news is that most people are endowed with a strong support system that could comprise a number of factors, such as strong family support, a circle of friends, emotional maturity, and an open and honest relationship with our parents (to name a few factors, among many).

In the wake of this theory, the dialogue turned from a rather black-and-white, reductionist framework that only had space for one factor being responsible for the cause of mental illness into a movement toward research that opened up space for the possibility of more than one cause. That is, it used to be believed that either nature (biology) or nurture (the environment in which a child was raised) was solely responsible for mental illness. But this is no longer the case: room has been made for a middle ground in which there could be more than one causal factor.

One of the leading theories that has expanded upon the model proposed by Meehl is sometimes referred to as the "differential susceptibility hypothesis," and was developed by J. Bilksy (Vaknin, 2020). It shares the assumption that there is a latent genetic vulnerability that is set into motion by various stressors; however, it suggests the possibility that mental illness can also be a useful adaptation in an environment that supports it (Vaknin, 2020). This is consistent with the theories of evolutionary biology mentioned earlier, according to which narcissism in an increasingly narcissistic environment would give an individual an edge over those who don't exhibit narcissistic tendencies.

With all the talk of the genes, the inevitable questions start to arise about the heritability of mental disorders. The burning question is, can they be passed down from one generation to another? The short answer is that there is really no definitive consensus about that (Grande, 2018). There is ongoing study in the field of epigenetics, which has revealed promising results for the future of understanding the ways in which phenotypes are transmitted intergenerationally (Grande, 2018). Essentially, what this means is that the genes themselves are not passed down, but rather the way we express or experience those genes is subject to change and subject to transmission from parent to child (Grande, 2018).

You can see from this chapter that, when it comes to understanding the etiology of narcissism, there are no clear answers. There is a set of detailed theories, though, and studies that lead us in the general direction of a clearer grasp of how narcissists come into being.

Behind the Smokescreen

Like the magician on stage, beyond the smoke and mirrors is an exceptionally well thought-out plan that involves deception and illusion. Using the power of stage presence and showmanship, you bear witness to more than your logical mind can fathom. In the same way, the narcissist wants you to behold the magnificence of themselves in all of their superhuman splendor.

You should, at this point, be able to give a comprehensive and in-depth account of what a narcissist is, if asked. Egocentric, charming at first, lacking in empathy...and the list goes on. You should be able to get into specific details about which type of narcissist does what, and maybe even provide an explanation as to why. Trying to establish the true thought process that drives the narcissistic machine is impossible if you are looking at the assemblage of verbal cues, facial expressions, and gestures that the narcissist supplies, as much of the time these actions can simply be the defense of an extremely fragile ego and identity and are not a true reflection of the real person behind the mask. In the last chapter, we looked beyond the mask of the narcissist into the deeper reality of what could be at the root cause of this set of character traits that isolate the narcissist emotionally from other people.

So, by now your knowledge of how the narcissist might act is rich in detail. You also have a greater understanding of the ways in which the narcissist's own body and troublesome past can both play a role in bringing their narcissistic character into being. Bearing witness to these factors in the make-up of your own spouse, this chapter seeks to lay out the untended wound that the narcissist carries with him or her. Seeing beyond the cruel exterior can help you to navigate your relationship with more understanding. Going beyond the mask and under the skin has so far revealed what appears to be the cold-blooded network of veins that somehow connect the wounded heart from childhood, the broken brain and genes that are susceptible to madness if prodded by the incorrect combination of a lack of protective factors and pressure from one or more stressors. If the make-up of the genes is vulnerable, they can only be pulled and prodded, stretched and squashed so many times before symptoms erupt like a volcano on Vesuvius or a storm about to break.

We will now revisit some defining traits of the narcissist and look at those characteristics through the lens of the perspective we have gleaned from previous chapters in an attempt to expose the nerves beneath what is portrayed as a thick skin. We will go through the main defining features of a narcissist that we have become acquainted with in this book and provide a deeper account that sees beyond the behavior in terms of personal history and the wound beneath the scar. Behind all of the following behavior, beyond the hurtful, irritating, exhausting, and confusing behavior of the narcissist is a person driven, on a level more fundamental than their limited insight allows, by a fragile ego that needs validation.

To start off with, we have mentioned the superficiality of the narcissist's relationships more than once already in this book so far. But why do relationships with narcissists tend to be one-dimensional? Despite your best efforts to create greater depth through connection and communication, your good intentions are fruitless. Don't take it personally, though; everyone the narcissist meets has the same problem. A narcissist's relationships with others—whether it is the postman, her parents, friends or you—are transactional. What this means to you in your everyday life is that you serve a purpose to the narcissist, as does everyone else in her life. Once you have fulfilled your purpose, you are dead weight and can be discarded. Whether it is in your emotional life or in the bedroom, your partner sees you as an object to be used for her own benefit. You may try to turn up the heat and create more intimacy in all aspects of your life, but this will prove futile.

Secondly, recall the way a narcissist tries to take the center stage, no matter the cost. This is her way of overcompensating for an extreme sense of loneliness. It also indicates that the narcissist has very low self-esteem and a low sense of self-worth. Most healthy adults are able to derive a sense of achievement from within themselves without depending on external validation from others.

Whether she is a vulnerable, grandiose, or malignant narcissist who is somatic or cerebral, covert or overt, narcissists don't like criticism. They balk at the thought that someone inferior to them should be telling them how to behave. Depending on the person and the timeline of their experiences as a child, it is possible that, by reacting defensively in response to criticism or diverting the conversation, they are protecting the fragile ego that arose as a result of childhood trauma. On the other hand, it could be the case that they would simply rather not take responsibility. Or they might just become emotionally reactive as memories of their critical parents judging them come to mind when you trigger them.

We have covered here a few of the traits discussed earlier in the book. Let us examine next the thought processes of the grandiose narcissist and vulnerable narcissist separately. In his YouTube video *What Are Narcissists Really Thinking* (2020b), Grande explains the inner thought process that might be going on behind the scenes of the narcissist's behavior. This section will recount the scenarios he describes, as well as the explanations he provides for the behaviors. The first scenario is if you are supposed to meet your wife for dinner and she arrives late intentionally. According to Grande (2020b), there could be a number of thought processes that justify this kind of behavior. She might think, for example, that her time is too valuable to waste—she had other things to do. Or she could be thinking that she won't be told what to do, or that she needs to demonstrate that she has power in that particular situation.

In another scenario that Grande (2020b) provides, imagine that you and your wife have a commitment to go to an event with friends. Your wife criticizes your choice of attire. What thought processes could be behind the comment on what you are wearing? She could be wanting to keep up appearances. Knowing what we know about the narcissist's appreciation of what she perceives to be a "high status," Grande (2020b) suggests that she wants to be elevated to that status as well, and dressing appropriately is a step in the right direction for her to achieve that goal. She will probably want to look good in front of her friends, and you are part of that image and need to play the part. The thought process here may be as follows: if my husband is attractive, others will be jealous of me, which makes me feel good about myself (Grande, 2020b).

The third example that Grande (2020b) provides (and provides an explanation for) is one of infidelity. Let's say your wife has an affair, which is not uncommon with narcissists, and lets you know about it. Going so far as to have an extramarital affair could be a way of informing you that they think they can have someone who is superior to you, in which case an insult would be implied, with the intention to make you feel bad about yourself (Grande, 2020b). It could also simply express a desire of your wife to be with the suitor in question, as well as a sheer disregard for you and your needs and expectations—a typically narcissist case of her thinking that she can have whatever she wants regardless of the implications for others. It could also be a form of validation that was required for her to feel appealing. Or, alternatively, it could be an extreme statement that is meant to make you jealous.

To paint another picture that could easily feature in any narcissistic relationship, that can give you a better idea of the thought process that could take place in the mind of the narcissist: think about a situation in which you were fighting with your wife and she accused you of being the cause of that argument, specifically because you are mentally unstable (Grande, 2020b). This is an effective example of gaslighting. Grande (2020b) suggests that the fear that arises in the narcissist here is that she will lose control of the relationship. If you turn out to win the argument, her dominant position over you will be put into question, and you will have a degree of power that she doesn't want you to have. On a broader and deeper level, she is aware that she has a problem and is at fault and tries desperately to hang on to her omnipotence by projecting her flaws onto you. She doesn't want you to be aware of this and blames you. The consequences of her behavior, in terms of how it affects you, are irrelevant.

For Grande's (2020b) fourth example, think of a time that you went out. You committed to being home at a certain time and mistakenly got back slightly later than expected. As soon as you walk in the door, your wife is questioning and criticizing you. She is angry and annoyed to the point that she is throwing insults at you. You have to wonder what could possibly be going through her mind that makes her emotionally reactive to what would be considered a perfectly human lapse of awareness of the clock when having a good time out with friends. The problem here could be one of a number of things. First off, we know that a narcissist's focus is on him- or herself. In this situation, the only thing that she can possibly think about is her needs and how she has been affected by your tardiness (and that should be your number one priority too) (Grande, 2020b). There may also be some degree of anxiety and insecurity that arises in her when you are out with others as well, as she is afraid that you will become less dependent on her and start to gain more control in the relationship (Grande, 2020b). Not only that, but you and her friends might gossip about her and they might provide insight to you that could expose her behavior and reveal her narcissistic ways (Grande, 2020b). This example highlights the pathological need for control and the potential thought process that might happen in the inner clockwork of the narcissist's mind.

Does your wife avoid engaging in deep topics of conversation? If this is the case (as it is with most narcissists), she may recognize that you want or need those kinds of conversations to happen, but she also is quite happy to simply reject your needs because hers are more important (Grande, 2020b). No matter what the reasoning she gives—whether she thinks she has better things to occupy herself with, or she is trying to make a point about her superficial nature—the point is that she will not compromise, or sacrifice her precious time to meet your needs.

Here is another example that Grande (2020b) gives, which doesn't refer to having an intimate relationship with a narcissist specifically, but you may be able to relate to it, as it can be quite common. You and your wife go to a restaurant, and your waiter makes a mistake with your order. Your wife lashes out at him. Her act might be justified by the thought that she is better than him, and that berating him makes her look better (which, naturally, she is, but other people should bear witness to this) (Grande, 2020b). This type of behavior can be seen in other contexts as well, for example in the workplace or in a social setting. The narcissist elevates her position, not by highlighting her own accomplishments or skills, but by putting others down (Grande, 2020b). If an onlooker is unable to see through the farce, it may very well appear that she is better than the person she is making look bad. Another reason why she might lambast the waiter is that she is overcompensating for feelings of insecurity.

Another bizarre example that Grande (2020b) provides is if your wife pretends to have a relationship with someone famous. First, she might simply want to affirm that she is special and make you agree in an energy-efficient way (i.e. it is easier for her to lie than convince you of her unwavering degree of specialness) (Grande, 2020b). The emphasis here is on the preference for ease and simplicity, rather than honesty. This reflects the broader lack of consideration for values that most people expect, and unspoken rules in society and relationships. The blame might tacitly be put onto you for failing to acknowledge how special she is, hence the need to lie.

This demonstrates the narcissist's need to project blame onto others to avoid taking responsibility for their own questionable behavior, even though they may be aware they are in the wrong. It may be an act of self-defense, a reluctance to justify her actions to anyone (Grande, 2020b). Or, if she genuinely believes that she is perfect, which she probably does, admitting to doing something wrong would be nonsensical (Grande, 2020b).

In another classic ploy of the narcissist, you might find that your wife is putting you down to your other family members, possibly behind your back. This may be part of a strategy that is employed to make you unlikeable to her or your family, which provides fertile ground for roping them in as part of the following, or harem, that is put together to support and validate the narcissist (Grande, 2020b).

The above scenarios describe situations that could likely occur with a grandiose narcissist. The previous chapter revealed that although the grandiose and vulnerable narcissist share the same core characteristics, they differ in the way that they exert control, and their methods of manipulation are also different. We will now take a look at the kinds of scenarios you might expect to arise in the life of a vulnerable or covert narcissist, and the deeper thought processes that could be happening.

Chapter three revealed that the vulnerable narcissist is extremely sensitive to criticism. If you, or anyone else for that matter, attempts to give her their opinion, she may deflect the criticism by reminding herself that she only values the opinion of people who have a high status, who are perhaps at least as amazing as she is. When in the line of fire from a critic, she may even attempt to turn the argument on you and start accusing you. The reality in this situation may easily be that she is, in fact, hurt by the criticism (Grande, 2020a). Instead of admitting this, expressing her vulnerability, and maybe reflecting on the criticism, she lashes out at you, thinking that it will make her feel better. And it does. Alternatively, criticism, she might say to herself, is only appropriate for those who are not perfect (Grande, 2020a).

The second possible scenario that is described by Grande (2020a), is if your wife falsely accuses you of something, then proceeds to take on the role of the victim. In this situation, Grande (2020a) suggests that what is happening here could be simply that she is unable to take being accused of something, although she is quite capable of doing the same to others, so she plays the victim. This shows her inability to take responsibility, and to put others down to make her look good. A second possible explanation is that she didn't plan for you to stand up for yourself in this situation, so she assumes victim status as an automatic way of responding (Grande, 2020a).

Another situation that happens often amongst narcissists is that they say something they shouldn't, then claim they don't remember ever saying it. This, according to Grande (2020a), could be a disappointing reaction even to the narcissist who would have preferred to invent an additional lie to cause more harm, but couldn't think of one. Alternatively, she might be aware that it is a case of he-said-she-said, so there is no harm to her for claiming not to remember as she knows that nobody in the office has the guts to question her (Grande, 2020a).

The covert narcissist is fond of bringing up topics that are sensitive to you out of the blue for the purpose of enjoying the sight of you experiencing emotional pain. The reason for this, says Grande (2020a) might be that she is feeling sad and wants you to feel sad as well. Or, she might be making you suffer out of spite, as revenge for one something you did in the past (Grande, 2020a). Finally, she might like to see you suffer and not be seen as directly responsible for the pain that is caused by your comment (Grande, 2020a).

Another classic situation that happens with vulnerable narcissists, especially at work, is that someone produces good work, and the narcissist takes it upon herself to take the credit. A narcissistic wife can do something similar. What could be going on here, suggests Grande (2020a), is that this act is motivated by anger that stems from the idea that she is better than the other person so her work should automatically be better. Or, she thinks that she could easily have done the same work of the same quality, and since it has been done by someone else, she can take the credit because she just as easily could have done it herself (Gande, 2020a). Thirdly, she might want some degree of credit because she gave the other person the work in the first place, and without her contribution, the other person would never have had the work (Grande, 2020a). This scenario exemplifies the tendency of the narcissist not to want to acknowledge the achievements of others.

You may recall that the victim of vulnerable narcissistic abuse constantly feels inadequate and like he is being showered with criticism. But, if your partner is launching an attack at you, the underlying motivation might be that, for example, it takes away her pain (Grande, 2020a). Her attacking you out of the blue for something trivial might also be a way for her to express her irritation at being around people she deems to be inferior (which includes basically everyone) (Grande, 2020a). It may also be a passive-aggressive way of trying to let you know that she has a need that is not being met, which requires you to read between the lines and figure out what is wrong or what she really wants (Grande, 2020a).

As another example that we can use to explain the sometimes mysterious actions of the narcissist, Grande (2020a) describes a situation in which a father suddenly ceases communication with his daughter. One of the explanations he gives for the narcissist doing this, in his opinion, is that he feels shame for not being a good father and prefers to take the easy route by cutting ties rather than dealing with the shame (Grande, 2020a). Another possibility is that he has given up after many years of hinting at the fact that she disappointed him, and she never responded to these hints (Grande, 2020a). Finally, Grande (2020a) suggests that the daughter may have done something in the past to offend or hurt the father and the father is proving to her that he naturally bears a grudge and accusing her of not knowing him well enough to know that. These last two possible explanations exemplify blame-shifting to avoid accountability.

In another example, Grande (2020a) describes the common habit of narcissists to advertise their earnings to people without mentioning the exact figures. Part of the reasoning behind wanting to share this information with people is that she wants people to know she is better than them, and that her superiority can be quantified (Grande, 2020a). Secondly, the narcissist recognizes that someone else is better than her in some ways, and wields information about her earnings as a way of trying to appear like she isn't (Grande, 2020a).

In the next scenario that Grande (2020a) describes, a narcissistic mother is giving her son the cold shoulder. This may be a passive-aggressive way of getting across her feelings of being hurt by the fact that her son is getting older and becoming more independent, and treating her son in this way may be the only way she knows to communicate her needs (Grande, 2020a).

The final example Grande (2020a) provides describes the vulnerable narcissist temporarily behaving in a confident, grandiose way in a group of people. They may be putting on a front, trying to appear as strong as they perceive a specific grandiose narcissist to be (Grande, 2020a). This act may also be designed to put on an act for others to see how powerful they are, which is sometimes a ploy to win people over to summon a harem that supports and validates them (Grande, 2020a). It may also be a way of overcompensating for their knowledge that they are weak—they try to prove to themselves that they can be strong (Grande, 2020a).

In any case, most of the typical strategies that the narcissist uses to deal with problems they encounter are immature and unhealthy reactions that emerge because, for one reason or another, they were not equipped with the knowledge of how to respond more appropriately and how to solve problems more effectively.

The aim of this chapter was to look beyond the smoke and mirrors to the person behind the smokescreen. We did this first by investigating the possible causes of narcissism in adulthood. We explored the relationship between the environment and childhood upbringing, and the possible role that brain structure and genetics could have in creating fertile ground for the development of pathological narcissism in adulthood. In light of what you have learned in this chapter and the previous chapter, it may be tempting to become sympathetic toward the narcissist to the point that you are moved to feel guilty or put your own needs aside. However, it ultimately comes down to the fact that, regardless of the cause of their behavior and whether or not they accept accountability for their reluctance to get help, they are responsible for themselves, as you are responsible for you.

Chapter 5:

Toward Still Waters

When you first started this book, you may have felt like you were in a sinking rowboat in the turbulent waters of confusion and loneliness. As you start the fifth chapter in this book, you are equipped with a vast supply of theoretical information from the previous chapters regarding the deep and often unpredictable territory that you are in. Even without the contents of chapter five, the information provided thus far sets you in good stead to be able to use that knowledge to navigate the stormy seas of the relationship you have with your narcissistic partner, or at least understand her better. The goal of this chapter and the next is to take it one step further and provide you with the practical tools and skills you will need to repair the boat. After reading these final two chapters, no matter what is happening around you, you will know that you can depend on your inner resources for navigation to a safer haven that is ultimately within your own heart and your relationship with yourself.

If you have been feeling like you have been thrashed around by the violent storm of narcissistic abuse, gasping for clarity amidst an unrelenting torrent of your spouse's unwanted opinion that constantly puts into question the legitimacy of your own experience, you are indeed in dangerous waters. 'Abuse' may seem like a strong word to use, even too strong for situations in which you are not emerging physically battered and bruised. Physical and sexual abuse are far easier to recognize and label than emotional, verbal, or psychological abuse, so using the word might seem like a daunting proposition.

The aim of this chapter is to help you to navigate the unchartered territory of creating a new story for yourself that requires you to put your money where your mouth is and step up. Beyond the narrative of the narcissist that paints you as the enemy, the weakling, or whatever derogatory term she wants to use against you, is a different story. There will be many challenges, one of which is to believe your own experiences and ascribe legitimacy to them. There is a very fine line between living with a narcissist and experiencing narcissistic abuse. Without the physical scars, it can be difficult to believe your own story, especially when there is a constant torrential downpour of accusations, snide comments, and insults that whittle your identity and self-confidence away. This is one of the reasons why it can sometimes be extremely difficult for people who are abused to leave. No matter how much they suffer, they don't believe that their own experiences bear any weight. It can be hard to argue with someone who is perfect. It may seem like it will come down to a case of he-said-she-said, with the odds stacked against you.

This chapter will help you to suspend the weight of all the accusations and ideas you have come to believe about yourself that have originated in the desperate mind of the narcissist. It will start by describing the long term effects of emotional abuse and go on to list the different stages of recovery that abuse survivors go through. It will then provide you with a clear idea of the red flags that you should look out for in determining how narcissistic your wife is, as well as a user-friendly checklist of narcissistic traits that can help you to determine where your wife is on the spectrum. After reading this chapter, you should also have some ideas of the different types of healing modalities that might be able to help with long-term recovery.

The Long-Term Effects of Narcissistic Abuse

We all know the images of the housewife who is beaten up, or the girlfriend who is sexually assaulted or raped. The violence is very much an overt, in-your-face kind of assault that others can testify to. It's hard to argue with bruises. But there is a more insidious kind of abuse too, that appears when words are laced with toxicity and selfish ill intent, one where your right to express yourself is trampled upon unscrupulously and your needs are discarded like worthless trash. Some of the definitions of abuse, according to Merriam-Webster (n.d.), include "language that condemns or vilifies, usually unjustly, intemperately and angrily" and "physical maltreatment." In addition to this, in the context of using the word as a verb, "abuse" is defined as ""to put to a wrong or improper use," "to use or treat so as to injure or damage," and "to attack in words."

Narcissistic abuse has long-term consequences for the victim. We have discussed the effect that it can have on children to some extent, but sharing years of your life with a narcissist can have a dire effect on anyone. Women have given accounts of the effects of narcissistic abuse in *Becoming the Narcissist's Worst Nightmare*, recounting how they experienced physical and sexual assault from their partners in addition to verbal abuse (Arabi, 2016). In these pages, they are clear about the way in which they reached a point where they could no longer trust themselves to make decisions, sometimes even giving up activities that they found meaningful to avoid being ridiculed. Some relay their experiences of how the abuse became more extreme over time, and how, toward the end, insults were essentially the only means by which their abusers communicated with them. An annihilation of self. Insecurity, lack of trust, depression, decline in physical and mental health, difficulty entering into trusting relationships with others...and the list goes on (Arabi, 2016).

From the above accounts, it becomes apparent that the underhanded abuse handed out by the narcissist can affect people's ability to function normally, both during the abuse and in the aftermath (let alone thrive). A lot of women mention suffering from Post-Traumatic Stress Disorder, or Complex Post-Traumatic Stress Disorder as a long-term effect of narcissistic abuse, and this is one clear way that verbal, emotional, and psychological abuse are so insidiously destructive and damaging in the long run (Arabi, 2016).

Most of the attention in the literature, and in therapy rooms, is given to Post-Traumatic Stress Disorder, and less time is spent on Complex PTSD. What differentiates the latter from the former is that symptoms of C-PTSD can arise when there is chronic trauma that occurs on a continuous basis. Narcissistic abuse is a case in point, especially for children who spend their early years in an abusive household, and cases where you are in a long-term abusive relationship with a narcissist.

Symptoms of Complex PTSD include the following, as laid out by Arabi (2016):

1. Flashbacks can take place that transport the victim back in time to the traumatic event, especially on an emotional level. Seemingly ordinary incidents in everyday life can trigger these, but they can cause a significant amount of distress.

2. Dreams are also affected by the strong emotionality associated with traumatic events. The way these dreams manifest is usually by individuals having nightmares about traumatic events happening.

3. The overdeveloped inner critic plays no small part in the mental chatter of someone who suffers from Complex Post-Traumatic Stress Disorder. A person with this disorder will be constantly judging themselves and failing to live up to their own standards. This may be an

internalization of the critic role that the narcissist played during the period of abuse.

4. Avoidance can be a major coping mechanism that is used to protect oneself from experiencing the recurring distressing symptoms of Complex PTSD. If an individual experiences flashbacks when a certain topic is raised in conversation, for example, they will avoid seeing people to avoid experiencing those flashbacks.

5. The scope or range of emotions of people with C-PTSD can be limited—this can be described as 'numbing,' where a person does not experience the depth of emotion that is considered normal (this can also be called "emotional flatness.")

6. Social anxiety can develop, usually as a by-product of feeling insecure or ashamed—these feelings have arisen as a by-product of months or years of experiencing a perpetual negative commentary from a narcissistic partner.

7. Noticeable hypervigilance and increased levels of anxiety can also feature with Complex PTSD. This can take form in a number of ways, including panic attacks, distrust and extreme emotions, and can affect a person's ability to concentrate.

8. Deeply embedded feelings of worthlessness are part and parcel of Complex PTSD that occurs in the aftermath of emotional abuse, which can

manifest as the desire to give up on oneself, taking the path of least resistance instead of self-care. These are rooted in feelings of shame and feeling like they are not good enough to deserve love and care.

9. Dissociation can feature here too. This is when a person feels split from their minds or bodies. In its most extreme form, Dissociative Identity Disorder, a person develops alter egos that they are not aware of and these different identities perform actions that the person can't remember doing.

10. Black and white thinking patterns might emerge. This can also be described as an 'all-or-nothing' mindset, in which perceptions or judgements are made that give no room for middle ground. This type of thinking can be applied to any person or situation, including themselves. For example, they might think that someone is either completely good or the sum of all evil—they have difficulty recognizing the complexity in a person or thing.

11. People with Complex Post Traumatic Stress Disorder might have distorted views of the person who has done them harm.

12. Sometimes victims engage in self-destructive acts like cutting themselves, binge-drinking, overspending, or other risky behaviors.

13. People who suffer from Complex PTSD could also have thoughts about killing themselves,

with feelings of hopelessness and sadness on an emotional level.

You can see above that continuing to perpetuate the unfairly balanced status quo in an abusive relationship can have dire consequences for the victim. To retain the victim role is beyond harmful, and there are measures you can take to "upset the applecart" and change the rules a little so that you are the one calling the shots. Your mental and physical health depend on it.

Stages of Recovery from Narcissistic Abuse

Reading this book is a step in the right direction toward gathering the knowledge, skills, and tools you need to take back control of your life and pursue a more meaningful and happier one. Hopefully it has already inspired you to seek other resources and start to network in order to build yourself a strong foundation of social support. When it comes to healing from narcissistic abuse, Arabi (2016) lists 11 stages that a victim of narcissistic abuse tends to go through on the journey to recovery:

1. Recognizing narcissistic behaviors and giving them the label of 'narcissistic'—this includes all behavior that is abusive and that can be pathologized. Don't forget that narcissism occurs on a scale, with NPD on the extreme end.

2. Putting a stop to assuming that the narcissist has the same value system and capacity for empathy that you do.

3. Choosing to validate your own truth rather than the narrative that has been created for you by your narcissistic partner through the various techniques that were mentioned in the first few chapters of this book.

4. Building a strong social network that you can rely on to hold you to your word.

5. Staying committed to reducing contact with your spouse, or stopping all contact with her. The ideal situation would be to eliminate all contact altogether, but circumstances sometimes don't allow for this.

6. Starting to engage in thorough self-care practices that help you to cultivate physical, emotional, mental, and spiritual health. You will learn about some excellent ideas for this in the next chapter.

7. Coming up with your own narrative that contradicts the one your wife has been perpetually playing in your ear.

8. Remembering your identity from before you were abused (and if there is no recollection of this, then identifying with a spiritual identity), and allowing yourself the space to grow.

9. Using a variety of healing modalities to heal from your self-destructive habits, such as self-sabotage and addictive tendencies. You will see

examples of this in this chapter, as well as in the final chapter of this book.

10. Using your experiences to help others—converting your victim story into that of the hero for the benefit of helping others in similar predicaments to overcome their circumstances and heal.

Hopefully by now you will have become acquainted (and maybe even well-versed) in some of the steps listed above. If, at this point in the book, you still have not identified the narcissistic, or even abusive qualities, in your wife, below you will find a final, concise description of the red flags that can serve as a clear warning sign that you are dealing with a narcissist, in no uncertain terms.

Red Flags

The kind of self-doubt that you have become intimate with is one of the most fundamental and problematic warning signs that you are living with a narcissist. If you are struggling to trust your own inner knowing, your own awareness of your feelings of powerlessness and frustration, then you have a problem on your hands. This can manifest as having difficulty expressing your truth to your partner, or others you are mutually acquainted with. If this is the case, you should definitely be hearing alarm bells. Of course, as you have seen, this factor alone doesn't warrant labeling your spouse as a narcissist, but it's definitely something to be aware of as you read up on some other warning signs which, when combined with this, may indicate that you are married to a narcissist. As you have seen in previous chapters, the icy grip of the narcissist that literally throttles your opinions and smothers your voice, freedom, and perhaps even thoughts can manifest in a variety of ways, depending on the type and subtype of narcissism involved.

One of the most obvious signs that your partner is a narcissist is the sharp contrast between the over-the-top love-bombing that may have initially lured you into the relationship, and the way you feel during devaluation stages. If your partner is a narcissist, it's been a steady decline from cloud nine to feeling completely worthless, drained, and used. As discussed elsewhere, this can take the form of a dramatic cycle throughout the relationship, wrenching you emotionally from elated feelings of being adored to feeling like you are never good enough and worthless. But it also typically takes the form of a gradual descent from the euphoric early stages of the relationship, via increasing levels of abuse, to being at your wits' end and desperate. Although at the beginning stage of the relationship you were showered with expressions of love, sex, compliments, and gifts, at this point in the relationship it is no longer necessary for the narcissist to do so as you have already been won, claimed as another trophy that can be exhibited to others—more proof of the sheer brilliance and unyielding power and success of the narcissist. If you were love-bombed in the early phases of your relationship, it is likely that such dewy-eyed attempts to woo you into her life have been on the decline and indeed no longer exist now that you have been lulled into complacency and unquestioning submission. You may, of course, still experience love-bombing in the aftermath of devaluation or belittling phases, and the occurrence of this gift-bestowing, compliment-heavy attempt to win your trust is another classic red flag.

Victims of narcissistic abuse are often at the mercy of the narcissist's changing moods and opinions. If you are living with one, you may find that her opinion of you is forever oscillating between an over-valuation of you and you being on the receiving end of constant criticism or the cold shoulder. Remember that this type of treatment plays no small role in creating the addictive element in the relationship—this hot/cold treatment triggers the release of the same chemicals that are involved in addiction to substances. This "intermittent reinforcement"—randomly giving out rewards for acceptable behavior in order to win someone over—keeps you obsessing over receiving the next reward, such that although your spouse might be treating you badly for most of the time, the supply of rewards keeps you hanging onto the expectation of the next reward, dulling your awareness of, or concern for, the way that she mistreats you.

Another red flag is if your wife gossips with other members of your family, or misrepresents you or your relationship. A classic example of the genius potential of narcissists to choreograph people to their own tune is in their love and perpetuation of gossip. While this may seem like a normal, trivial function of life in the social world, there is an element of skulduggery involved in a relationship with a narcissist that, to put it plainly, is not designed to work in your favor. On the contrary, narcissists like to use people like pawns in a chess game, where you are the king being cornered with little room for maneuvering. The tidbits of information you think you are entrusting to your spouse end up turning into weapons that can be used against you, and the same applies to anyone who falls into the trap of thinking they can confide in the narcissist. This is true for the truths that you share with them about your insecurities or weakness, as well as your strengths, skills, and attributes. The feelings that you share about parts of yourself that you don't like, or things you have done in the past that you feel bad about, could be used against you at any time in the future. Likewise, things you are proud of might be used to butter you up one day, and the next it will somehow be converted to an insult that is used for the sole purpose of bringing you down. In this cat-and-mouse game, nobody is safe except for the narcissist and sadly, you are the one who feels the brunt of this shameless manipulation as your wife is the person you are supposed to confide in and trust more than anyone. The narcissist likes playing the victim if that is what it takes to get attention, and doing this sometimes requires painting you in a bad light, unfortunately for you. This may be part of the larger intention to build up a harem that supports the narcissist by consolidating the almost heroic narrative that she wants to create for her own security and validation, and makes it impossible for you to express your truth and feel secure, validated, and supported within your family and circle of friends.

Furthermore, if you are in a relationship with a narcissist, the green-eyed monster of jealousy is an unmistakable presence that is inevitably lurking in one place or another in your household, once you start paying attention to it. If you entered your marriage with a child from another partner, for example, you may notice that your wife exhibits jealousy toward him or her because they are a threat to her and may distract you from what she considers the real object of your attention—herself. We saw in the chapter that spoke about the causes of NPD that growing up with a narcissistic parent can have adverse effects on your child, as her jealousy will necessarily affect the way she treats him or her. Growing up in a family with a narcissistic parent can have damaging effects on the healthy psychosocial development of the child. Your wife may also accuse you of being unfaithful and exhibit an exaggerated sense of jealousy toward the person you are allegedly having an affair with. Your spouse may fly off the rails and into a "narcissistic rage" publically, when she finds you with someone of the opposite sex. These traits are especially applicable to the grandiose narcissist.

Jealousy can be directed toward you as well, and might not be so easy to recognize. The narcissist may use your achievements to advertise her success in having a partner like you, but have a latent resentment for your accomplishments that is not shown publicly. When nobody is watching, she might minimize the importance of what you have achieved. Jealousy may also be present in your relationship in the form of what may feel like a permanent state of competition. If you feel the need to have something you are proud of celebrated by your partner, you can forget about it— she is probably more likely to use it as a springboard to flaunt her own achievements and downplay yours. This competitive streak has a way of converting fun activities, like board games, into a sinister (and highly draining) battle of the ego. Your spouse might even make it her business to sabotage you to prevent you from achieving something by putting you down before a meeting, distracting you from work while you are preparing for a presentation, or planning a party for the night before you have an exam. Another classic maneuver that should make you doubt the authenticity of your wife's support is if she treated your goals with an unmistakably condescending attitude.

Be on the lookout for attempts by your wife to invoke jealousy in you as well, by talking about ex-lovers to try to make you feel insecure or jealous. This only serves to keep you wasting energy on earning your place in your current relationship, which you should by no means need to do. If you fall for this trap, your sense of self-worth is dependent on the relationship. We will reinforce in the next chapter, the emphasis on developing and trusting a solid sense of self that can make you respond fearlessly in holding your ground in situations like this, and in the way you conduct your life moving forward in general. Like a bully poking fun at one of the unpopular kids, this behavior is to try to elicit a reaction from you or keep you groveling for attention. It does not reflect a loving relationship and takes advantage of your own codependent tendencies.

With most narcissists, relationships are mostly transactional. Their relationship with you is no exception! This means that you serve a particular purpose for the narcissist - if you want depth and emotional maturity from your narcissistic spouse, you've got the wrong person. In their never-ending quest for high status, power and respect from others, narcissists tend to go for attractive partners. You have gathered by now that if you know a narcissist, expect to be manipulated, especially if it means his cunning tactics get you to stay in the relationship (recall the section on love-bombing, intermittent reward and addiction).

If you are still unsure whether your wife meets the criteria of being a narcissist, you can use the following set of questions to help gain clarity. The following checklist is adapted from *Psychology Today* (*Is Your Partner a Narcissist?*, 2014). It emphasizes that NPD is a spectrum disorder, and that the more affirmative answers you have, the more likely it is that your partner has full-blown NPD.

1. When things don't go according to plan, does your partner avoid taking the blame?

2. Does your wife divert responsibility for her own behavior?

3. Is your wife under the impression that she always knows all the answers?

4. Does your spouse exhibit an inability to identify how you or your children are feeling?

5. Is your partner's number one priority, when it comes to relating to you and your children, how your and their behavior reflects upon her?

6. Does your partner seem to be out of touch with her own feelings or seem to deny them?

7. Does your wife have a tendency to hold a grudge?

8. Does your wife make everything about her?

9. Does your partner lack the capacity to listen to you?

10. Does your partner have a habit of trying to control your behavior?

11. Do you feel like you are inadequate, based on the messages your partner has been sending to you?

12. Is your spouse never interested in hearing about you in conversation?

13. Does your wife talk a lot about herself in a positive light and talk a lot about you in a negative light?

14. Do you often notice that your partner is lying?

15. Is she manipulative?

16. Have you observed your partner changing her account of events to make herself look good, according to who is listening?

17. Does your partner judge your kids according to what they do, instead of who she understands them to be?

18. Do your kids show a reluctance to spend time with your wife despite loving her?

19. Do you think that your children hold back from expressing their feelings with your partner in order to protect themselves?

20. Is your wife generally distrustful of other people?

21. Do your kids spend a lot of time trying to win the approval of your partner?

22. Does your partner not spend a lot of time with the kids?

23. Does your wife, more often than not, prefer not to go to the kids' events because she is not interested in them?

24. Does your wife stop your kids from doing things they enjoy and encourage them to do things she is interested in instead?

25. Have you had feedback from other people that reflects that they think something about your partner is out of the ordinary?

26. Does your wife exploit others?

27. Is your wife controlling and is power very important to her?

28. Is your wife preoccupied with the image that is presented to others?

29. Does your wife seem to have a flexible, inconsistent, or nonexistent value system that informs her behavior?

30. If you are divorced, does it seem as though your wife still wants to take advantage of you?

31. When you and your spouse are talking about a problem you in particular are having, does she divert the conversation to the topic of her own issues?

32. If you are communicating about how you feel, do you get the sense that your wife is trying to outdo your feelings?

33. Do you get the impression that your wife has a sense of jealousy towards you?

34. To the best of your knowledge, is your partner unable to feel empathy?

35. Does your wife have a tendency to show support for objects, people, events, or institutions that make her look good?

36. Does your partner have an emotionally distant relationship with you?

37. Do you regularly wonder whether your wife loves you?

38. Is your spouse only nice to you when other people are close by to see it?

39. When you are going through a difficult time (e.g. there has been a death in your family), is your partner's first reaction concerned with whether this will have an adverse effect on her?

40. Does your wife care too much about what other people think?

41. Does your wife take advantage of you?

42. Do you feel like it is your fault when your wife becomes sick?

43. Do you sometimes doubt whether you are acceptable to your spouse?

44. Have you noticed that your wife is overly critical of other people, including you, and can be quite judgemental?

45. Do you get a sense that your wife is not interested in knowing who you really are?

46. Does your wife have an inflated sense of self-importance, and is she egotistical?

47. Does your spouse sometimes seem like she is not genuine?

48. Does your partner tend to oscillate between depression and a state of grandiosity?

49. Does your marriage often seem like it is a competition?

50. Does your wife like to have things go exactly how she wants them to?

If there was any doubt before, you should now be certain about whether your suspicions about your wife being a narcissist were correct. Being at the receiving end of the multitude of different types of narcissistic behavior can be abrasive to your soul, especially if you are in an intimate relationship with a narcissist. The reason why narcissists are sometimes referred to as "energy vampires" becomes apparent from the feeling that victims of narcissists describe as having the lifeblood sucked out of them. This feeling comes from living in an environment that is characterized by the constant presence of fear and anxiety. It's no wonder that you have reached a point where you can no longer tolerate it and are seeking solutions. We will discuss these here, in the context of long term recovery from abuse, and in more depth in chapter six.

Recovering From Abuse

In the next chapter, we will deal with the possibility of following the exit signs and making a U-turn by cutting ties with your partner and committing to the policy of having absolutely no contact with her. We will also discuss the types of things you can do to stay sane, happy, and healthy within the relationship in case, for whatever reason, you decide to stay. However, being abused by a narcissist can form scars that can last for many years. The good news is that, as is the case with any wound, tending to it properly can help it to heal.

To do this, you may need to get creative about the kind of support you seek. Books and resources such as this one, not to mention a solid network of people who understand you, will provide a good foundation, but you may find that you need to be active about getting more help and treatment, and doing requires ongoing commitment to the process. This can include mainstream approaches suggested by Arabi (2016), like Cognitive Behavioral Therapy or group therapy, for example. Cognitive Behavioral Therapy is a short-term therapeutic approach that has proved to be highly effective in treating a number of disorders, and it can be used to change flawed thinking patterns that may have arisen as a result of the incessant insults launched at you by your wife, not to mention all the other forms of attack she may have implemented against you. It is very goal-oriented and requires a hands-on approach from you, in terms of activities for you to do at home. Group therapy is also a good idea, as it puts you in touch with and allows you to share experiences with people who can relate to your pain. You can share your story without worrying about being judged, and listen to those of others. Some victims of emotional, psychological, or verbal abuse find it difficult to express themselves using language, so art or music therapy can be highly effective in enabling them to find self-expression through visual or performing arts therapy (Arabi, 2016).

You could opt to choose a more alternative approach, which are vast in number, and come from a wide variety of sources across the world. Most, however, are practiced all over the world, thanks to the explosion of information across the world in recent decades. The best thing to do is to research ones that resonate with you, and follow through with the ones that you think could help. Below are some alternative approaches that Arabi (2016) suggests.

Mindfulness meditation is a practice that hundreds of thousands of people all over the world use to practice being present. Studies have been done to show that, with enough time and practice, the brain can be rewired and long-term commitment can result in physical changes in the brain, which have an effect on depression and anxiety. This once again reminds us of the plastic nature of the brain that was so important for the development of the emotionally and mentally healthy child growing up, and is equally important to remember for a person trying to heal from trauma resulting from narcissistic abuse.

Mindfulness meditation can be as simple or as complicated as you like, but beginners meditations usually focus on something simple like the breath. You can take 20 minutes of your day to start training yourself to keep bringing your attention back to the present moment, but mindfulness is a way of life that can help you to return to yourself in your everyday life. Through this practice, you can find more peace and groundedness. According to Arabi (2016), it can help trauma survivors to practice being more present and proactive than reactive, and can help people suffering from PTSD to distinguish real threats from perceived threats. There are other meditations you can do as well, that are focused on particular topics, such as building your confidence or cultivating gratitude, which can do wonders in broadening your perspective and simply changing your beliefs. Meditation is a very powerful healing practice.

Reiki is another modality that Arabi (2016) recommends. It is a form of energy healing that originated in the East, and is used to help balance your energy and clear blockages. It is based on the assumption that your energy body is intimately connected to your mental, physical, and emotional state, and can help you to move through the healing process on an energetic level, which will affect your overall health.

There are other healing modalities that work with energy, such as chakra balancing and cord cutting (Arabi, 2016). Chakras are seen, in some cultures and belief systems, to be energy centers that are associated with different parts of your body, that can sometimes be out of balance. Restoring this balance is seen to be significant in maintaining health. Cord cutting is a ritual you perform of meditation that enables you to sever ties with someone you are in a toxic relationship with.

There are a number of other activities you can do or healing methods you can use to heal your mind, body, and soul after being in an abusive relationship, though you should bear in mind that recovering from emotional abuse can take decades. Some of these activities include yoga, acupuncture, neuro-linguistic programming, and hypnosis (Arabi, 2016). Spending time in nature is a great way for you to get some peace and quiet, where you can take some time to process what you have been through at your own pace, relax, and get some perspective (Arabi, 2016). And it's free.

We started this chapter with reference to the analogy of the boat. It may still seem to be sinking now, but this chapter has begun to provide you with the practical tools and working knowledge you need to repair your boat and find safe harbor. Now that you have gained some clarity about narcissistic abuse, acknowledged the red flags, and worked through the checklist in this chapter, in the next chapter you will be provided with some indispensable tools that can help you to make different choices moving forward.

Chapter 6:

Playing the Game

So, you find yourself trapped in a story that no longer works for you, one in which you have the short end of the stick. It's a story in which you are the brunt of cruel jokes and endless manipulations, and you are like putty in the hands of an unrelenting antagonist who is out to get you for her own pleasure or gain. You are suffering, feel constantly drained, and are tired of walking on eggshells. Well, at the end of it, you've finally realized that you are married to an incontrovertible and incorrigible narcissist who refuses to relinquish the reins and surrender dominion of your own mind and being. You have, at last, realized that there is another way, that you can encourage the release of her hold on you, and that you don't have to suffer through it alone on the same projected path as you were headed. Period. Unlike Narcissus, or any other character in the fairy tales, your story is still being written, and it can be one of resilience, strength, empowerment, and heroism.

So far, your wife has set the rules in her cat-and-mouse game, and you have obliged to submit to her inflexible, uncompromising rulebook and instruction manual at great cost to you. But, as you have realized as you have read this book, there are ways and means that you can beat her at her own game and take responsibility for your sanity. This is not necessarily achieved by returning the immature tactics employed by your partner, but rather to adopt the mask of parental figure for yourself as you learn to make more responsible choices in the face of a very destructive addiction.

This chapter serves as your own instruction manual for the way forward, as you relearn or forge a new pathway that can keep you out of the firing line and help you to dodge the bullets of abuse. It won't be easy, and perseverance is key. You will find that as you practice the methods suggested in this chapter, it will not only become easier to establish a new status quo in your relationship, but also that you will start to develop an insurmountable strength that is like no other. This is the ultimate lesson that you can take from a narcissist: she gives you the fuel to become unshakably resolute and intimately acquainted with yourself, if you dare to take up the challenge. You will learn, through your healing process, to become immune to other people's opinions, and might indeed end up looking like the bad guy (but this time you will earn your reputation!). Through this process, you will need to learn to let go of your attachments.

You have two options. The first option is to take a U-turn in the relationship. This requires making the executive decision to cease all contact with your wife. This may seem like an extreme option, nigh on impossible at this point, but many people vouch for this course of action, and it can ultimately be the most effective if you want to live a life that is not ruled by a dictator. And, if the well-being and security of you and your family is at stake, this may be the only option. Arabi (2016) emphasizes that this may be the more difficult choice, given the addictive nature of a relationship with an abuser, but that is for you to decide once you read more about the pros and cons of taking such an approach and what it entails, compared to what the second approach would ask of you.

The second option (and this may be the only possibility for some, depending on your circumstances) is to stay in the relationship and learn how to hack narcissism. After talking about what the "no contact" method entails, this chapter will provide information regarding how you can best navigate living with a narcissist, assuming that you don't take the approach of completely cutting ties with your partner. This will take the form of discussing how you can most effectively respond in situations where you feel triggered into acting emotionally. It will also address the topic of open communication that reflects your growing ability to mindfully return to your grounded authentic self, even in the midst of a narcissistic storm. It will touch on classic mistakes that you should try to avoid making in order to avoid aggravating an already volatile situation. In addition to this, a few common-sense self care tips will be provided as a way of providing a substantial bedrock upon which you can build your new life and self.

No Contact

There is no mystery as to this approach to resolving your problems with a narcissist. Deciding to eliminate contact with the narcissist means severing all contact and communication with the person, removing yourself completely from the relationship and any connection with the offending person. There are, of course, the obvious ways of severing ties with a person, like not seeing them or calling them. This includes communication on social media, apps, and emails...even asking mutual friends and acquaintances about her is totally out of the question (Arabi, 2016). Not only is there a risk of triangulation occurring, but by doing this, you run the risk of being triggered or returning to the cycle of addictive behavior that will have you back at square one and back in the relationship in no time, only to begin the excruciating process of leaving once again (Arabi, 2016).

Then there are the not-so-obvious things. For example, you should stop going to the favorite haunts that your spouse likes to frequent—shopping centers, restaurants, you name it (Arabi, 2016). Bumping into your partner is not worth the risk as it is an unnecessary cause of distress. You can also go so far as to remove items and objects from your home that remind you of her (Arabi, 2016). Arabi (2016) also recommends that you stop having contact with mutual friends because if they haven't already been enlisted as members of the harem, they will be once you break contact with your partner!

The point of taking this approach is to create a life for yourself that is no longer attached to your spouse, so that you don't continue to create more trauma for yourself. By eliminating the possibility of getting lured back into the relationship through the manipulations of the narcissist, there is no opportunity for your wife to trigger you. If you even open the door for triangulation to happen, for example, by initiating contact with the narcissist, you are allowing yourself to walk freely into her sticky clutches and return to the cycle of abuse all over again.

Choosing the path no contact provides you with the space and perspective that you deserve, without being harassed by the incessant abuse from your partner. It allows the clouds to part and the waters to calm. It frees up your energy and time, allowing you to focus on moving forward with your own life, instead of wasting energy on keeping your head above water in the turbulent waters of an abusive relationship. With this newfound space, you can set your sights on you and your future instead of drowning in a maelstrom of unwanted projections from the narcissist in your life.

You'd be making a mistake to think that the path of no contact is easy. As pointed out by Arabi (2016), there are a host of important factors that make breaking up with a narcissist exponentially more difficult than breaking up with an ordinary partner. But if it does seem daunting, imagine a life for yourself where you have the space to achieve your goals, spend time doing things you have always wanted to do and that you enjoy, pursue healthy relationships, and recover from the trauma caused by months or years of abuse (Arabi, 2016).

In *Becoming a Narcissist's Worst Nightmare*, Arabi (2016) suggests five ways you can call it off with your partner, to the extent that your circumstances allow. The first method is to go "cold turkey"—to leave your spouse without giving her a heads-up. You've realized she is a narcissist—now leave, without falling back into the trap of self doubt, before you become entangled once again. Pack your bags, change your phone number, and walk out the door. This has particular challenges of its own, such as not having a pre-planned place of residence.

To some, this may seem like an impossible feat, especially if you are not the only one who is involved, or if there is another factor that ties you to your spouse. You might have joint commitments, for example, like a shared property or business (Arabi, 2016). If this is the case, you can take another approach. You can still terminate the relationship, but you can take it slower so long as you ensure that you don't lose your conviction along the way (Arabi, 2016). This approach still entails leaving, but allows you the time to plan ahead. Make sure, once you have decided to leave, that you start creating more space for yourself in the meantime, taking the time you need to look after yourself so that you can make clear-headed decisions and plans (Arabi, 2016). You might want to start saving money, for example, and make sure you have the support you need, whatever form that may take. Arabi (2016) warns that your wife may notice a change in your behavior, start to suspect that you are preparing to leave, and shift into fifth gear in her attempt to keep you in her sticky clutches. Don't be tempted, don't be swayed. You can stand in the certainty of your conviction, like a rock in a raging river, and look after yourself during this time by taking some time to yourself every now and then.

Another method that can be used is described by Arabi (2016) as the "last straw" method. If you use this method, you may have a burning desire to leave, but feel as though you need extra incentive, one final incident or event to push you out the door once and for all. You know you are going to leave and are mentally prepared for it; it is simply a question of when. You are keeping track of what is going on in the relationship, maybe by taking short notes about every incident that occurs, keeping yourself aware and on your toes all the time, because you intend to leave and won't allow yourself to slip back into complacency (Arabi, 2016). You may find it useful here, as you gain momentum toward walking out that door by taking one or two dramatic steps from which you can't return (Arabi, 2016). You might, for example, confide in a friend about the problems you are having with your partner.

In certain circumstances, it is not possible to cut ties with your spouse completely (if you have children, for example). An effective alternative is to use the well-known approach called the "Gray Rock Method," so called because your behavior here is intended to be as unremarkable as a gray stone in a cairn of gray stones. It is described on a blog called *The Gray Rock Method of Dealing with Psychopaths* (2018), as follows. The term alludes to the way you should fade into the background while still contacting your partner where it is unavoidable, thereby ceasing to be the source of drama that your spouse has depended upon for her fix of supply. This blog describes how, by abstaining from supplying the drama by responding to your spouse in the most mind-numbingly boring way, your partner is pretty likely to lose interest in continuing to use you as a source of supply, simply because you are insufficiently interesting to her. Remember that a narcissist gets bored easily, so if you respond to messages about trivial things in the most excruciatingly detailed way, no doubt she will look for better candidates to supply the required entertainment. This approach is best used for a malignant narcissist (or psychopath), and is a great option if going no contact is not an option (*The Gray Rock Method of Dealing with Psychopaths*, 2018).

The final method suggested in *Becoming the Narcissist's Worst Nightmare* (2016) is more of a short-term way of dealing with a narcissistic person in your life, than a long-term solution. It involves being openly clear about what you will and will not tolerate, no matter what it takes. It could mean that you dig your heels in and remain unresponsive to taunting, or it could mean correcting everything that the narcissist says about you. It could mean walking away from intolerable situations and, as Arabi (2016) emphasizes, it requires that you do walk away if your spouse oversteps the line. You may even find that she soon loses interest in you and finds herself someone else who will be more tolerant of her manipulations and lies.

So, how do you know if you should cut ties with your partner completely, or not? Some people argue that choosing to take the approach of no contact is the optimal choice for anyone, but if the well-being of your family is under threat, it is the only option that is available. What does it mean to be under threat, exactly? This refers to more than physical well-being, in the sense of the absence of physical abuse. Think of safety on a broader level, encompassing any threat to stability or wellness on a physical, social, emotional, or psychological level. Activities that could be considered a threat might include the following if they are performed by your wife on a pervasive basis. If your wife engages in these activities (among others), then you might do well to consider removing yourself and your family from the situation entirely (Arabi, 2016):

- refuses to get a job
- gambles or spends money excessively
- drives after having been drinking
- evades taxes
- threatens you, herself, or your children

Severing ties with a person you have a toxic relationship with can be more difficult than learning how to adapt and find effective solutions to living with them. This is because, as we mentioned in chapter one, being in a relationship with a narcissist can be likened to an addiction; it has been said that it stimulates the same hormones that are stimulated in drug addicts. The only difference is that you are addicted to your partner and the unpredictable chaos in your relationship. When you start implementing the no-contact approach, you may experience withdrawal. This may inspire you to impulsively initiate contact with your partner again—this is a bad idea, because it can cause even more trauma, and you may be tempted to continue the relationship.

You will be glad to know that you can prevent withdrawal and promote similarly high levels of the abovementioned chemicals by doing other things instead of making contact with your partner, or subjecting yourself to the highs and lows you have come to associate with being with her. Arabi (2016) recommends you do some of the following to provide you with the levels of chemicals that your body has become used to due to your addiction:

1. The following activities can help create feelings of intimacy, love, caring and comfort that are associated with high levels of oxytocin.

- Be more generous toward yourself, and toward others.

- Spend more time with friends.

- Do something nice for someone more frequently.

- Meditate—it can help to increase self-love.

- Have more physical contact with others and animals. If you have pets, cuddle them, or else volunteer at an animal shelter. Start hugging friends and family more. And, if you are ready, you may find it useful to start a casual romantic relationship with someone new.

2. Do more activities that get your adrenaline pumping, such as skydiving or white water rafting. The possibilities are endless! Doing things like this means you won't have to rely on your partner to provide you with adrenaline-inducing behavior.

3. Do things that give you a sense of accomplishment, like starting new projects or getting a new job that you love. It doesn't matter how big or small the tasks are—set yourself a challenge and be inspired to do your best and conquer your demons of self-doubt. This can help you to feel rewarded without

depending on the narcissist to give you a sense of reward through intermittent reinforcement that keeps you addicted. Ignite your passion for life by doing things that make you feel excited, and that put you on a path toward greater things that can help you to build an enthusiastic, positive energy that makes you look forward to life.

4. Write an ambitious bucket list and follow through spontaneously, and be sure to include things on your list that challenge and excite you. Include activities you have never done before, just for the sake of curiosity.

5. Go out with friends who genuinely care about you.

6. Go out by yourself. Do something that you enjoy by taking a day every now and then to yourself. Spend a day at the beach, go see a movie, or treat yourself to a meal at your favorite restaurant. Don't be afraid to try new things as well. This will help you to build a bank of memories in which you have positive experiences of being by yourself, and the recognition that you don't have to be with your narcissistic partner in order to have fun and do things you find pleasant. You will begin to realize that life can be whole and complete without being in a relationship with another person, never mind one who brings endless amounts of toxicity and pain to your life.

7. Laughing more, forcing yourself to smile even when you don't want to, and doing yoga have all been shown to help decrease cortisol levels. Introduce more humor into your life by watching more comedy shows, for example.

8. Listen to a variety of music, especially music that helps you to feel the anger that might emerge in the days and weeks following the difficult relationship you have had with your spouse, especially if it has been bordering on abusive.

Can you picture the overdone social media posts and cliched signs hanging in gift shop windows instructing you to "laugh often, love deeply, and dance like no one is watching"? It may be embarrassing to surrender to the wisdom hidden in these gimmicky commands. Do them, though.

As you contemplate the possibility of establishing no contact and saying 'adios' to your narcissistic partner, don't forget the value that lies within establishing a support system. Taking the no-contact approach is essentially like trying to stop taking drugs and, as any addict will know, this cannot be done without the necessary social support. While rehab is not an option for a person recovering from narcissistic abuse, there are plenty of other options available out there. For support groups to therapy, to your friends and the plethora of information you have at your fingertips, use your resources efficiently to find all the help you can get.

Living With a Narcissist

Some people would argue that electing to pursue the "no contact" approach is the more difficult option, taking into account the addictive quality of a relationship with a narcissist. The alternative is learning the ways and means by which you can train yourself to beat the narcissist at her own game, by your own self-development.

Now, before we get into the specific things you can do to make life better for yourself when in the company of a narcissist, it should be pointed out that your behavior can sometimes add fuel to the fire of the narcissist's onslaught. Your own traits can sometimes attract a narcissist into your life and make it easier for them to abuse and exploit you. There is a nugget of truth in the statement that narcissists are particularly attracted to people who are sensitive and who have a lot of empathy.

Above and beyond that, by virtue of the fact that you are a human being, one of the most instinctive ways of responding when you are being verbally bludgeoned to smithereens by your partner is the "fight, flight, or freeze" response. Everyone has a reflexive way of reacting to perceived danger. One of the unavoidable knee-jerk reactions that we all have inherited on a primal level is the way we respond to dangerous situations. We are all predisposed to reacting to what we see as threatening situations by either fighting back, fleeing from the situation, or freezing. What I want to highlight is that this reactive response can work against you (and probably has up until now) but that, with intention and practice, you can harness these reactions to work in your favor and take better control of the situation.

Sometimes these three primal responses can exacerbate tense situations with the narcissist, and can even make you easy prey. Behary (2013) gives some advice about how you can turn these kinds of situations around and defuse the conflict. If you are a person who tends to respond by wanting to fight back instead of getting aggressive, you can retain a sense and intention of self-defense without making it personal, and thus add fuel to the fire. Behary (2013) suggests using wording like "I won't tolerate being treated so disrespectfully. If you are uncomfortable with me, you can tell me without putting me down or ignoring me...I'd appreciate it if you could speak to me with more consideration, and I'll do the same for you." If you are the kind of person who avoids conflict situations, instead of running away in a panic, you can recognize that you need some time to yourself and try to remove yourself from the situation by being honest about it: "I need some time to regroup and gather my thoughts so our conversation might be productive" (Behary, 2013). When you return, you will feel more confident about your ability to speak your truth, and at the same time more mentally prepared with a response. People who freeze in such situations feel naturally inclined to take the path of least resistance and end up agreeing with the narcissist (Behary, 2013). Recognize this, and just be honest about this by saying something like "I get triggered by these exchanges, but I'm working to strengthen my confidence. I'd appreciate it if you could be more thoughtful toward me. You have responsibilities in this relationship too" (Behary, 2013).

The key here is effective, honest communication, rather than submitting to habitual reactions and emotional responses that reflect your past conditioning. Bear in mind, particularly if you are a fighter, that there is nothing that a narcissist dislikes more than being wrong. There is every possibility that any point you make during an argument is bound to fall on deaf ears. If you are going to try to get a point across, try to make out as if it was her idea, or persuade her to reach the point you want to make without actually making it yourself. When you are having an altercation with a narcissist, you may feel a burning desire to beat her at her own game by arguing against her. We've seen that the narcissist allows no space for the opinions of others, so trying to give her a piece of her own accusatory medicine is not a productive route to take. However, you may find a glimmer of hope if you try to convince her of your point of view as though she is reaching the same conclusion you were wanting to make—except that in this case, she would believe it was her point all along, which naturally would make it more agreeable.

According to Behary (2013), the key to being successful in this endeavor of improving your communication skills when you are in a tight spot that causes you to react physically and respond reactively, and indeed in having to live with a narcissist, is to be mindful. If you can practice being present and grounded in how you feel each and every day, you are already one step ahead of your old self and one step closer to embodying a more authentic you in the face of an energetic and verbal onslaught.

By practicing staying grounded when you are amongst people in everyday life, and when you are around your wife, you can start to lay out boundaries for yourself that can help make life more pleasant. According to Arabi (2016), you can do this by:

1. Saying 'no' to things you don't feel comfortable agreeing to. Although doing this may seem selfish at first, you know yourself better than anyone and have every right to decline from doing something you don't want to, without having to explain yourself to your partner.

2. Ceasing to look for approval from others and finding your own sense of self-worth instead of relying on others to validate you.

3. Speaking your truth when you feel cornered or bullied. Don't revert to reactive tendencies that make the problem worse. Practice being present with how you feel and expressing how you feel verbally, especially in the thick of an emotionally charged or tense moment—it will get easier with time.

4. Cultivate a sense of humor and don't take the narcissist so seriously—this is exactly what she wants. If you can shrug off the actions and words that are created to pierce you like a barrage of arrows, much of the malicious energy will not be received by you and will dissipate.

5. Start taking classes in a physical activity that can help you to release angry energy that you may be bottling up as a result of difficult relationships or bullying that you may have been victim to.

These are all part of a self-care regimen that should go well beyond weekly martial arts classes, and there are plenty more where those came from if you get creative and listen to your physical and emotional self and trust your intuition. Self-care should be your number one priority. It should include but not be limited to the above suggestions, as well as some way of spending time by yourself, whether it is through taking a stroll, spending time in nature, meditating, jogging, writing, listening to music, or engaging in your favorite hobby, for example.

By switching the priority from ensuring that you are good enough for your partner (which you never will be, simply by virtue of the fact that she is a narcissist), to recognizing the need to look after yourself as a human being with physical, spiritual, emotional, and mental needs and learn how to address them through research, trial and error, and connecting with others in a similar situation. I will re-emphasize the need here for community support and building a network for yourself of people who can relate to your experiences, who can confirm that they are unacceptable and that you deserve better, who can offer you the resources you will need, and who can provide you with moral support and a sense of genuine belonging.

Common Mistakes

Along with the aforementioned tips and tricks that can help you to be the captain of your own ship and navigate the uncertain waters of your relationship, you will also benefit from knowing the sorts of things victims of narcissistic abuse tend to do often, that simply make things worse. You can avoid making those same mistakes by side-stepping the traps that are waiting for you to fall into.

If you remember the method of 'triangulation' that was described earlier in the book, you will recall that narcissists have a habit of manipulating other people to take their side, of fabricating truths that align to the most heroic version of themselves, without considering how this might affect you (who is sometimes portrayed as the villain in the story), in order to reap all the attention. Believe it or not, this triangulation could include people you have asked to be present in a confrontation with the narcissist, who you thought might be of assistance in giving you some support. For this reason, Sayers (2018) recommends that you don't involve others if you choose to address your concerns to the narcissist, no matter how loving or diplomatic you intend to be, and regardless of how close you are to that person. It could backfire.

Secondly, as tempting as it may be to unveil your newfound knowledge of narcissism and allocate the label openly to your wife to her face, this is definitely not advisable (Sayers, 2018). Why? A typical narcissist might recognize the genius behind this approach and try the same maneuver on you, accusing you of being of unsound mind by referring to all sorts of disorders. Not only could this be totally ineffective, it could really just make things worse, especially if it starts a new narrative in the narcissist's mind that she can use as the basis of a brand new smear campaign which could alienate you further (Sayers, 2018).

Another thing that is suggested by Sayers (2018) in *Energy Vampires* is that you should be careful not to allow your emotions get the better of you, even (or especially) when you are triggered by a narcissist. This makes you vulnerable, as a narcissist can tell when you are feeling this way and will probably add insult to injury by making a flippant comment about it in order to whittle the remaining scrap of confidence that is left in you down to nothing. In times like these, you should also get into the habit of owning and making peace with your emotions (remember how narcissists can make you doubt yourself?). Use the advice provided in the section about self care to ensure that you do not make this mistake.

Co-Parenting With a Narcissist

Now you know the options, in terms of moving forward with your life and taking care of yourself, and you are equipped with the knowledge and advice you need to do so effectively. But what if you have children with a narcissist? This can make matters exponentially more complex. It can be a more difficult feat than navigating the situation without kids. More often than not, having children together means that you will probably remain in contact with your wife, especially if she retains custody. The same advice that was provided in chapter five and in this chapter applies here in order for you to better take care of yourself and manage communication, but on top of that, Arabi (2016) provides some very useful tips for co-parenting with a narcissist:

1. Decide not to answer the phone. If you are still burdened with the idea that you are at the beck and call of your partner at your own expense, let go of that idea. You have every right not to answer the phone when your wife is calling you, especially when you know what her motives are. You can give yourself permission to answer or not, and with any luck she will leave a voice message and you can think about your response before you do.

2. Get a new phone number and ask for email communication instead. To put it simply, the fewer means of contacting you that your wife has, the less opportunity there is for drama and harassment. It's not a crime to change your phone number, and requesting email communication decreases the likelihood that she will contact you unnecessarily. You can even ask the court to supervise this email communication. Set up your email on your phone so that you can access it anywhere and respond immediately if it is urgent. Keeping record of communication becomes easier if you only have one method of correspondence.

3. Don't allow her inside your house. You have a right to a safe environment where you live—this is one of the reasons you left the relationship, remember?

4. Don't feel obliged to move your schedule around because she can't be bothered to stick to her parenting obligations. If you have a visiting schedule set up for the kids, there is no reason why you have to agree to requests to change it if something better comes up for your wife. Get a doctor's note if she claims she is sick.

5. Keep a record of everything, and I mean everything. Keep evidence of your communication, and record every time she doesn't follow through with her commitments and if there is any sign that your children have any kind of physical injury when they return from visiting your wife.

6. Let go of attachment to what happens when your children are visiting your partner and accept that this is something that you can't control. Stay positive and do what you need to do to stay sane while they are away. This can include putting happy pictures of your kids on the wall, setting positive intentions, and plastering the walls of your house with positive affirmations.

7. Don't talk negatively about your spouse around your children—this can create a world of pain for them. Focus on being a good, grounded

parent. If you need to vent, ask a trusted friend to listen, but make sure that your kids are not within earshot.

At the end of the day, you choose your story: are you going to keep treading water, struggling for survival and sanity, or are you going to embrace the challenge and own your story by empowering yourself with the knowledge and support you need to stay afloat and take the journey of your choosing? Recall that the eighth step in the journey to recovery from narcissistic abuse involved expanding your perspective to include a wider spiritual view, or even a return to the vision of who you were before the abuse. Cultivating a spiritual life is imperative to healing—indeed, it is a core element of any of the 12-step programs for addiction. We create our own realities, and yours can be greater than the dense, heavy energy that is confined to the relationship you have with your wife and the small world that she creates on your behalf. Take the profound teaching she gives you by simply being present in your life, and forge a positive future for yourself using the angry energy provided by your experiences with her to find purpose, meaning, and goals by growing spiritually. When things once seemed as hopeless as a sinking rowboat adrift in stormy seas, you realize that you do actually have the tools you need, and you have the strength within yourself to overcome the odds.

A note on abuse: if you suspect that you or a loved one are being emotionally, verbally, psychologically, physically or sexually abused, you should get help immediately by calling your local hotline or going to a support group.

Conclusion

Now that you have made it to the end of this book, you should have a crystal-clear theoretical grasp of some of the current theory surrounding narcissism, its causes, and Narcissistic Personality Disorder. At the same time, through the questions raised in this book, you have hopefully engaged in some dialogue with yourself and with others who have had similar experiences to determine whether or not your spouse is, after all, a narcissist. Besides benefitting from the process and knowledge provided in this book, you should also have a well-equipped arsenal at your disposal of practical strategies that you can use to defend yourself in sticky situations. Instead of playing the victim, you can use these techniques to fend off the narcissist traits you can identify in your wife and gain a greater sense of peace and well-being in your everyday life. You can do this by applying particular strategies when caught in a narcissistic maelstrom of verbal abuse, as well as by practicing a solid daily regimen of self-care rituals and activities that can help to keep your sanity intact.

There are those who say that the people who trigger us, who push our buttons, have the most valuable lessons to teach us. At the end of it, the one who challenges us most, who grinds us down to a pulp, gives us the raw material to create a beautiful self—one who can stand his ground, set boundaries, and move into other, better relationships with the ability to stay grounded. When we are confronted with desperation and have no choice but to depend on ourselves and heal, that's the sweet spot from which the most spectacular flower can bloom.

Arabi (2016) clearly points out that people with a history of being a victim of narcissistic abuse as children are more likely to perpetuate the pattern in their adult lives, at least until they can recognize that pattern and take appropriate measures to heal. If you haven't, repeating the pattern can further deepen the trauma and you will continue to get yourself into these tight spots for the rest of your life. So if you suspect you are in a relationship with a narcissist, and it is causing you to suffer, you should seek help. This book has equipped you with the knowledge and information you need to start your journey to recovery so that you don't repeat the same patterns throughout your life.

There are a number of psychological tools that can help set you in good stead of a long journey of physical, emotional, and spiritual healing. One of the important things to remember when you are recovering from narcissistic abuse is that you may end up looking like the bad guy, and your narcissistic spouse will definitely rub your nose in your change of disposition and choices. You may end up feeling guilty for saying 'no,' putting your spouse in her place, or choosing to put your interests before hers.

As Arabi (2016) reminds us, when living with a narcissist, your boundaries become permeable. The narcissist will take advantage of any leeway that is given. The onus is on you to choose whether to break contact for good, or to continue the relationship, but either way, you will have to draw a line in the sand and set your own boundaries, because nobody else is going to do it for you.

It is hoped that, by engaging with the material in this way, you have begun your journey along a pathway to a greater sense of self-love, self-empowerment and freedom. May your path be embellished with the finest, shiniest of paving stones and your tread in the world light as you apply the tools and techniques you have learned here to create a better life for yourself and for those you care about.

PS: If you enjoyed this book and feel that it made a valuable impact on your life, don't hesitate to share what you liked about it on an Amazon review!

References

Arabi, S. (2016). *Becoming the Narcissist's Nightmare: How to Devalue and Discard the Narcissist While Supplying Yourself.* Shahida Arabi.

Author Unknown. Diagnostic and Statistical Manual of Disorders. (2013). American Psychiatric Association. Fifth edition.

Behary, W. T. (2013). *Disarming the Narcissist: Surviving and Thriving with the Self-Absorbed.* Second Edition. New Harbinger Publications.

Cox, L. (2019). Covert Narcissism. Escape the Narcissist.

DavidJohn. (2018). 3 Different Types of Narcissistic Personality Disorder. **https://www.thenarcissisticabuser.com/dif ferent-types-narcissistic-personality-disorder/**.

Doctor Ramani. (2020, October 27). Cerebral Narcissists: What to Look Out For. [Video]. Youtube. **https://www.youtube.com/watch?v=zrpjD IRnQH4**.

Genetic and Environmental Contributions to Dimensions of Personality Disorder. (1993). *The*

American Journal of Psychiatry, Volume 150 (12), 1826-1831. **https://doi.org/10.1176/ajp.150.12.1826**.

Grande, T. (2018, March, 14). What Causes Narcissistic Personality Disorder? [video] . Youtube. Retrieved from **https://www.youtube.com/watch?v=5cK4z4cYQLY**.

Grande, T. (2019a, April 21). 10 Signs of Grandiose Narcissistic Abuse. [Video]. Youtube. **https://www.youtube.com/watch?v=I__sTf0-gtE**

Grande, T. (2019b, April 30). 10 Signs of Vulnerable Narcissistic Abuse. [Video]. Youtube. **https://www.youtube.com/watch?v=tEd6x0l3b6U**.

Grande, T. (2019c, June 8). Malignant Narcissism: Is It Narcissism and Psychopathy Together? **https://www.youtube.com/watch?v=JP0oTFxYo_U**.

Grande, T. (2020a, February, 4). *Thoughts of a Vulnerable Narcissist: 10 Covert Narcissistic Behaviors and Corresponding Thoughts.* [Video]. Youtube. **https://www.youtube.com/watch?v=cb9SyOQ2zAU**.

Grande, T. (2020b, January 15). *What Are Narcissists Really Thinking? 10 Narcissistic Behaviors and the Thoughts That Cause Them.* [Video]. Youtube.

Retrieved from **https://www.youtube.com/watch?v=YUuT ibVp6Vs**.

Guarino, G. M. (n.d.). The Different Types of Narcissism. **https://www.psychpoint.com/mental-health/articles/the-different-types-of-narcissism/**.

McBride, K. (2014). *Is Your Partner a Narcissist? Here are 50 Ways to Tell.* **https://www.psychologytoday.com/us/blo g/the-legacy-distorted-love/201412/is-your-partner-narcissist-here-are-50-ways-tell**. Retrieved from Psychology Today.

Merriam-Webster. (n.d.). Abuse. In Merriam-Webster from **https://www.merriam-webster.com/dictionary/abuse**

Merriam-Webster. (n.d.). Narcissism. In Merriam-Webster.com dictionary from **https://www.merriam-webster.com/dictionary/narcissism**

Narcissism. (n.d.) **https://www.psychologytoday.com/us/bas ics/narcissism**.

Pincus, A. L. and Roche, M. J. (2011). Narcissistic Grandiosity and Narcissistic Vulnerability in The Handbook of Narcissism and Narcissistic Personality Disorder. Campbell, W. K., and Miller, J. D. (eds). John Wiley and Sons, Inc.

Sayers, T. (2018). *Energy Vampires: How to Protect Yourself from Toxic People with Narcissistic Tendencies.*

Skylar. (2012-2018). *The Gray Rock Method of Dealing with Psychopaths.* **https://180rule.com/the-gray-rock-method-of-dealing-with-psychopaths/**. Retrieved from 180 Rule.

Vaknin, S. (2014, May 3) Somatic Narcissist: Not Sex, but Pursuit and Conquest. [Video]. Youtube. **https://www.youtube.com/watch?v=1dJFp AjOX0U**.

Vaknin, S. (2020, August 18). *Is Narcissism Hereditary, Acquired or Epigenetic? (Diathesis-Stress Models).* [Video]. Youtube. Retrieved from **https://www.youtube.com/watch?v=aEp-54xtqjo**.

Webber, R. (2016). Meet the Real Narcissists (They're Not What You Think). **https://www.psychologytoday.com/us/articles/201609/meet-the-real-narcissists-theyre-not-what-you-think**.